# Ambedkarism

# Ambedkarism

## Essays on Select Economic and Cultural Issues

**Praveen K. Jadhav**

RAWAT PUBLICATIONS
Jaipur • New Delhi • Bangalore • Hyderabad • Guwahati

ISBN 978-81-316-0327-7





*Published by*
Prem Rawat for **Rawat Publications**
Satyam Apts, Sector 3, Jawahar Nagar, Jaipur 302 004 (India)
Phone: 0141 265 1748/7006 Fax: 0141 265 1748
E-mail: info@rawatbooks.com
Website: www.rawatbooks.com

*New Delhi Office*
4858/24, Ansari Road, Daryaganj, New Delhi 110 002
Phone: 011 2326 3290

*Also at Bangalore, Hyderabad and Guwahati*

Typeset by Rawat Computers, Jaipur
Printed at Chaman Enterprises, New Delhi

*Dedicated to the memory of*

**Bharat Ratna Dr Babasaheb Ambedkar**

*for his great contribution*

*to Indian economy*

# Contents

# Preface

B.R. Ambedkar was a versatile personality. He was a sociologist, an economist, a political scientist and an expert in law. Besides, he was a great leader of the masses. His contribution to Indian sociology, economics, politics and law has been immense. He has analysed the Indian society in different contexts. His thoughts have brought revolutionary changes in the society, especially among the Scheduled Castes. He wanted to protect and promote the social and economic equality in India. In this direction, he organized a number of agitations, wrote books and delivered speeches. On the whole, his work has been quite remarkable.

Besides these, he was a perfect economist too. In fact, his first major academic work was in economics. He analysed a number of basic economic issues. In this context, he wrote *The Administration and Finance of East India Company* (1915), *Provincial Decentralisation of Imperial Finance in British India* (1921), *The Problem of the Rupee: Its Origin and Solution* (1922), etc. Further, he has also contributed a lot to the fields of sociology, politics and law as well. The book titled, *The States and Minorities* (1947) was an important contribution. He wanted to bring social and economic equality through state socialism. For this he propounded a model of economic development. However, the state socialism was not accepted as Ambedkar was expecting. However, in the post- independence period, many of his thoughts were accepted and implemented. But his thoughts on agriculture were not implemented. As a consequence of this, the system has come to serious setbacks in the contemporary period. Similar situation could be found in case of industries. The present book deals with select economic and cultural thoughts of Ambedkar and their relevance in the contemporary times.

According to Ambedkarites, Ambedkar's contribution has been revolutionary. He passed away fifty-four years ago but his thoughts are still alive and have been inspiring crores of peoples. The Ambedkarites in India, especially in Maharashtra, are living with his memory and the thoughts. They have developed their separate identity as Buddhists and are following a different cultural identity. This book tries to explain the Ambedkarites' activities as they represent a distinct culture.

Since Ambedkar's contribution to Indian society has been indeed considerable, it is difficult to portray it in one or a few book(s). There are innumerable books written by scholars, yet there is much more to be written. Recently, Sukhadeo Thorat (2008) wrote on Ambedkar's thoughts on the water policy. Actually, Ambedkar's thoughts cover a wide spectrum of issues; hence, it was difficult for me to deal with select thoughts. However, I have tried my best to explain the selected thoughts of Ambedkar and their relevance in the contemporary times.

In the first chapter of the book, the life and mission of Ambedkar has been explained. In the next two chapters, I have analysed Ambedkar's thoughts on agriculture and their relevance to the present times. In India, agricultural land has been divided into unequal measures. Ambedkar wanted to redistribute it through the state socialism, i.e., by nationalisation of agricultural land and redistributing it without referring the caste and religion. But since it was not accepted, it has resulted into a number of serious problems. In the later of part of the book, I have discussed the thoughts of Ambedkar on industries and their applicability today. I also have discussed the reservation and social exclusion issues with reference to Ambedkarism. In the last part, I have presented the Ambedkarites' tributes to Chaityabhoomi – the place, where Ambedkar was cremated. This discussion shows the Ambedkarites' apostrophe culture and activities on the occasion of his death anniversary.

The most important part of this book is the discussion about the development of Buddhists in Maharashtra. This has been viewed with the help of select samples from Mumbai. They also can be called Ambedkarites or the neo-Buddhists. They are the examples of the success of Ambedkarism. There is a perfect positive relation between Ambedkarism and the development of the neo-Buddhists. I do understand that there are a number of dimensions which are left out in the analysis. It was impossible to cover all the aspects within the compass of a single book. I am sure, this book will be of some use and benefit for the researchers, policy makers and other readers.

In writing this book, I must express my sense of gratitude to the memory of Dr B.R. Ambedkar for remaining an inspiration for me. Of course, Ambedkar's contribution is so remarkable and valuable that it has been inspirational for a large number of people.

I must express my sincere thanks to my father, late Shri Kempanna Ramchandra Jadhav, who wanted me to work on Ambedkar's ideology. I also express my gratitude to my mother Shakuntala for her kind support throughout my life. I must thank my brothers Sunil, Sanjay and Niteen, my sisters Vandana and Rajshekhar, and brother-in-law Anand, for their cooperation. I also thank my father-in-law Shri Jaysing and mother-in-law late Rekha for their moral support.

This work would have been impossible without the support and cooperation of my wife, Asavari. She always encouraged me to do everything, what I liked. Besides this, she also gave a number of suggestions on various matters. During this exercise, I cannot forget my children Siddhant and Pranjal, who have shown an unbelievable maturity and cooperation to me.

I have to express my thanks to Dr Deepak Tilak, Vice-Chancellor, Tilak Maharashtra University, Pune and Dr Umesh Keskar, Registrar, Tilak Maharashtra University, Pune for providing me with an academic environment in the university.

I must thank my teachers including late Dr R.R. Doshi, Dr J.F. Patil, Dr Vasant Jugale, Dr Ramesh Dandge, Dr Vijay Kakde (all of Kolhapur), Dr Kunda Damle (Pune), Dr P.N. Gawade (Kolhapur), Dr Katti (Kolhapur) and others. I also thank my friends Dr Prakash Kamble (Kolhapur), Dr A.G. Pujari (Mangalwedha), Dr Harsha Jagzap (Pune), Dr Jagan Karade (Pune), Dr Manik Sonavane (Pune), Dr Deepak Deshpande (Bhilwadi), Dr Shraddha Kumbhojkar (Pune), Mrs Jyoti Patil (Pune), Vishal Jadhav (Pune), Shahaji Kamble (Kolhapur), Shantinath Bhivashikar (Kolhapur), Vijay Kamble (Kolhapur), Satish Gavane (Sangola), Milind Dixit (Kolhapur), Subodh Mane (Kolhapur), Hemchandra Khopade (Pune), Yuvaraj Pasare (Kagal), Jeetendra Sawant (Kagal), Jeetendra Kamble (Pune), Dadarao Ingle (Pune) and others. I also thank Mr Hile, Miss Sanghamitra, Mrs

Sharmila, Mrs Shende, Mrs Pandit and all non-teaching and library staff of Tilak Maharashtra University, Pune.

I do understand that it is difficult to name everyone here. But I express my thanks to all those who have helped and encouraged me directly and indirectly. I also thank my friend Gajanan Gharge for typesetting.

Last but not the least, I am thankful to Rawat Publications, Jaipur for publishing this manuscript in its present form.

# Chapter 1

# The Life and Mission of B.R. Ambedkar

Babasaheb Ambedkar was a myriad-minded person, with expert knowledge in diverse disciplines. He was a social reformer, an educationist, a humanist, an economist, a sociologist, a political scientist, and a constitution-maker. He was responsible for the revival of Buddhism in India in modern times. Such a personality has been very rare in the Indian history. Ambedkar fought against the system for equality and freedom for the untouchables in India. The thoughts and activities carried out by Ambedkar were revolutionary. Although, the life and activities of Ambedkar cannot be presented in a few pages, yet an attempt is made to highlight some select moments of his life and activities in this chapter.

A large number of scholars have written about the life and mission of Ambedkar. Of them, Dhananjay Keer's book *Ambedkar: Life and Mission* (first published in 1954; third edition in 1971) is the most important. This chapter is drawn mainly from this book though some other books have also been consulted.

## Childhood and Youth of Ambedkar

The Ambedkars belong to Konkan Maharashtra in India. B.R. Ambedkar's ancestral village is Ambavade in Ratnagiri district. Ambedkar's grandfather, Maloji Sakpal came from a Mahar family. Maloji was a retired military man. Of his children only two survived, one was Ramji and the other was a daughter named Mira. Ramji Sakpal (the father of Ambedkar) had fourteen children. Bhimrao alias Babasaheb was the fourteenth child, born on 14th April 1891 at Mhow in Central Provinces. When Bhim was two-year old, his father retired from military service and came down to Dapoli, a small town in Konkan Maharashtra. Bhim began his primary schooling at Dapoli. But for the reason of job, Ramji Sakpal moved to Satara with his family. At Satara, Bhimabai, wife of Ramji and mother of Bhim, expired. In the later period, a good number of children of Ramji died. Out of fourteen children of Ramji, only three sons and two daughters survived. Balaram, Anandrao, Manjula, Tulsi and the youngest was Bhim. Bhim completed his primary education and began his high school career along with his elder brother at Satara. The stigma of untouchability was realised and faced by Bhim during his school days. He went through a number of incidents backed by untouchability. There was a Brahmin teacher in the high school, named Ambedkar. He loved Bhim since he was intelligent. Bhim was earlier known as Bhimrao Ambavadekar. The surname was given from his native place. The teacher changed Bhim's surname from 'Ambavadekar' to 'Ambedkar' in the school records. He gave him his own surname and Bhim was then known as Bhimrao Ambedkar.

Meanwhile, Subhedar Ramji shifted his family to Bombay and lived in a chawl called Dabak Chawl at Lower Parel. Bhim continued his studies in Maratha High School at Bombay. He showed a keen interest in reading a variety of books. After a few months, Bhim was sent to Elphinstone High School, Bombay. He studied hard and in the year 1907, passed the matriculation examination. This event was very special and rare and hence was celebrated by his community. Later, a meeting was called wherein, a well-known Marathi author and social reformer, Krishnaji Keluskar was present. He gave a copy of his new book, *Life of Goutama Buddha* to Ambedkar. After passing the matriculation examination, at the age of 17 years, Bhim alias Bhimrao married Rami alias Ramabai at Byculla Market, Bombay.

For the college studies, Bhimrao Ambedkar joined Elphinstone College, Bombay. During his college days, he again came across a number of incidents displaying untouchability. But Bhimrao continued his study. In the year 1912, he passed his B.A. examination. The boy from untouchable caste passing B.A. was a rare case – at that time. After his graduation, Bhimrao Ambedkar joined service in Baroda – the state of his benefactor. He was appointed as a Lieutenant in the Baroda State Forces. At this post, he could serve the state for about 15 days in January 1913. Here, he received a telegram from Bombay about the serious illness of his father. He left Baroda immediately. On 2nd February 1913, his father Subhedar Maloji Sakpal passed away. It was the saddest day in the life of Bhimrao Ambedkar.

## Educational Achievements of Ambedkar

After the death of his father, Bhimrao decided to face the situation with courage and was preparing to return to Baroda. Meanwhile, In June 1913, the Maharaja of Baroda had given an advertisement about sending some students to United States of America (USA) for higher studies. Bhimrao came across this advertisement and narrated his story to the Maharaja in his palace in Bombay. The Maharaja decided to send Bhimrao for higher studies at Columbia University, USA. On June 4, 1913, Bhimrao signed an agreement before the Deputy Minister for Education of the Baroda State and left India in the third week of July 1913 for USA. In America, he could read, write, walk, bathe and rest with a status of equality. In India, he had obtained his B.A. degree with English and Persian languages; but now he took up political science, moral philosophy, anthropology, sociology and economics as the subjects for his study. In the year 1915, he obtained his M.A. degree for his thesis, 'Ancient Indian Commerce'. In May 1916, he read a paper on 'Castes in India: Their Mechanism, Genesis and Development' in an anthropology seminar. Simultaneously, Ambedkar submitted his thesis titled, 'National Dividend of India: A Historic and Analytical Study'. In the second week of June 1916, the Columbia University accepted the thesis and Bhimrao was awarded the degree of Doctor of Philosophy (Ph.D.). This was the biggest educational achievement in the life of Bhimrao Ambedkar (in the later period, the thesis was published by P.S. King & Sons Ltd., London). This thesis was dedicated to His Highness Sayajirao Gaikwad, the Maharaja of Baroda. Ambedkar's thirst for the books was increasing. In New York, he purchased about two thousand old books. In June 1916, he left Columbia University, USA and reached London, UK to study law and economics. In October 1916, he was admitted to London School of Economics and Political Science. Bhimrao Ambedkar was working on a thesis for D.Sc., but in the meanwhile, he was informed that the period of scholarship was over and, therefore, he was called back to India by the Dewan of Baroda. Ambedkar had to return India without completing the study at London. On August 21, 1917, he reached Bombay.

According to the agreement, Ambedkar was to serve the Baroda State for ten years. The Maharaja wanted to appoint him as Finance Minister after he had gained some experience in the administration of different departments. So, he was immediately appointed military secretary to the Maharaja. At his office, he came across a number of incidents showing behaviour of untouchability. Ambedkar was treated by his staff and peons as a leper. One day, a group of Parsees came to him, and asked to vacate instantly the place where he was staying. Ambedkar had to leave the place. No Hindu, no Muslim would give him shelter in the city. He sent a note to the Maharaja, but there could not be any alternative arrangement in this matter. Finally, with helpless mood and utterly disgusted with the insulting environments, Ambedkar returned to Bombay in the middle of November 1917.

In November 1918, the government appointed Ambedkar as a Professor in Sydenham College, Bombay. The job was on a temporary basis. Ambedkar accepted this so as to accumulate enough funds to enable him to go to London to complete his studies in law and economics. The young professor with his fine dress, his profound studies, his serious glowing eyes soon became well known in the circle of students of economics. But here also, Ambedkar came across a number of incidents exhibiting signs of untouchability from the professors. At last, Ambedkar saved some money, got some help from the Maharaja of Kolhapur and took a loan of Rs 5,000 from his friend (Naval Bhathena) and finally left for London in July 1920 to complete his studies in law and economics. Meanwhile, the first and second sons of Ambedkar died in infancy, despite that, Ambedkar wanted to complete his studies. In September 1920, Ambedkar resumed his studies at the London School of Economics and Political Science and also kept terms for the Bar at the Grays Inn. During his stay at London, he used to go to Museum Library to read. He continued his research and read a large variety of books. He was the first person to enter the library and he was the last person to leave. He read the books by Marx, Lenin, etc. Although, Ambedkar was in London, but he was keeping himself well informed about the position of untouchables in India.

Ambedkar was a thorough academician. He made his highest educational development. He began his education from an ordinary public school from a small village Dapoli and reached a reputed university in America and England. At every time, he did not compromise on quality. He worked hard and obtained a number of degrees. He served on number highly designated posts in India. The most important contribution of Ambedkar was his writings. He wrote a number of books in the fields of sociology, economics, politics, anthropology, law, etc. His books were highly researched and had been in demand in many countries. Even in the contemporary period, there has been a significant demand for the books written by Ambedkar. Above all, he also established a number of colleges for educational development of SCs and others. C.D. Naik (2003: 332–36) has compiled the achievements of Ambedkar in following way:

### *Educational*

1897 Primary education at Dapoli School in the Konkan Maharashtra.

1907 Matriculation from Elphinstone High School, Bombay.

1912 Graduated from Elphinstone College, Bombay.

1915 M.A. with economics, political science, anthropology, sociology and moral philosophy. The dissertation on Ancient Indian Commerce or Administration and Finance of East India Company at Columbia University, USA.

1920 Resumed his studies at London School of Economics in London.

1922 Studies at Bonn University, West Germany.

1945 Founded his cherished educational establishment – the People's Education Society, Bombay.

1946 Founded Siddhartha College.

1950 Founded Milind College at Aurangabad.

1956 Intended to start an institute for legislature training to the young SC students. Founded Siddharth College of Law.

## *Positions Held*

1913 Lieutenant in Baroda State Force.

1917 Military Secretary to Maharaja of Baroda.

1918 Professor of Political Economics at Sydenham College of Commerce and Economics, Bombay.

1919 Practised at Bombay High Court.

1928 Took up professorship at the Government Law College, Bombay.

1931 Made Justice of Peace by the Government of Bombay.

1934 Professor (part time) at the Government Law College, Bombay.

1935 Principal of the Government Law College, Bombay.

## *Writings*

1918 Reviewed Bertrand Russell's *The Principle of Reconstruction of Society* and said that, it was not a book on peace as generally constructed. He also wrote on "Small Holdings in India and their Remedies" in the *Journal of Indian Economic Society*, Vol. I.

1933 Wrote a treat on Indian army.

1936 Delivered a speech, which was later brought out in a book form entitled *An Annihilation of Caste*.

1939 Wrote *Federation versus Freedom* stating how federation checks freedom.

1940 Wrote *Pakistan or Partition of India or Thoughts of India*, published by Thacker & Co., Bombay.

1943 Wrote *Mr Gandhi and the Emancipation of the Untouchables* (Thacker & Co., Bombay).

1943 Wrote on "Urgency of Industrialisation of India" (*Times of India*, 26th October).

1943 Wrote "Post-war Development of Electric Power in India" (*Indian Information*, 15th November).

1945 Published *What Congress and Gandhi have done to the Untouchables*, by Thacker & Co., Bombay. His other work was on *Communal Deadlock and Way to Solve It*, F&O Printing, Delhi.

1946 Published *Mahatma and the World*, by Thacker & Co., Bombay. Another work was on *Who Were the Sudras*, also by Thacker & Co., Bombay.

1947 *States and Minorities* was published by Thacker & Co., Bombay.

1948 His research entitled *The Untouchables* was published by Amrit Book Co., New Delhi. His work on *Linguistic Province and Maharashtra as a Linguistic Province State* was published by Thacker & Co., Bombay.

1950 The booklet on "The Buddha and the Future of his Religion" appeared in the *Maha Bodhi* journal, Calcutta, Vol. 58, April-May. His other brochure "The Rise and Fall of Hindu Women" was published by the *Maha Bodhi* journal, Calcutta in June.

1951 In *Revolution and Counter Revolution*, he analysed Indian history as nothing but struggle between secular forces like Buddhism, Jainism, Kabeer Panth, Krantiveer Phule and reactionary forces of caste and class.

1953 Published "The Need for Checks and Balances".

1954 Published *Riddles of Hinduism*.

1957 Published *Gandhi and Gandhism*. His magnum opus, *The Buddha and His Dhamma* was published by Peoples' Education Society, Siddharth College, Bombay.

### *Degrees and Dissertations*

1915 Dissertation on *Ancient Indian Commerce or Administration and Finance of East India Company*, at Columbia University, USA.

1916 Read a paper on "Castes in India: Their Mechanism, Genesis and Development" at Anthropological Seminar of Dr Goldenweiseer, published in *Indian Antiquary*, Vol. XII, May 1917, New York. Ph.D. on the thesis "National Dividend of India: A Historic and Analytical Study" at Columbia University, USA and published in 1924 as *The Evolution of Provincial Finance in British India: A Study in the Provincial Decentralisation of Imperial Finance*. by P.S. King & Sons Ltd., London in 1925.

1917 Ph.D. degree was awarded by Columbia University, New York.

1921 M.Sc. dissertation on "Provincial Decentralisation of Imperial Finance in British India".

1922 D.Sc. thesis on *The Problems of the Rupee: Its Origin and its Solution* was submitted to London School of Economics and Political Science, London, and later published by P.S. King and Sons Ltd., London in 1923.

Ambedkar also founded a number of educational establishments, especially for the backward castes. He established The People's Education Society at Bombay in 1945. Under this, he established a number of colleges such as Siddharth

College, Bombay (1946), Milind College, Aurangabad (1950), Siddharth College of Law, Bombay (1956), etc. Ambedkar focused mainly on the educational development of Scheduled Castes and Scheduled Tribes. The educational establishments of Ambedkar benefited the backward people a lot.

## Social and Political Activities of Ambedkar

In the year 1919, Ambedkar came in closer contact with the Maharaja of Kolhapur, Chhatrapati Shahu Maharaj. With the financial assistance provided by the Maharaja, Ambedkar started a fortnightly paper titled, *Mook Nayak* on 31st January 1920. Writing on inequality and discrimination, he said that the backwardness of the non-Brahmins was due to lack of education and power. In another article, he wrote that 'the good state must guarantee the equal status in matters, religious, social, economic and political, to all the classes'. On 21st March 1920, Ambedkar presided over a conference of the untouchables at Mangaon in the Kolhapur State, which was attended by Chhatrapati Shahu Maharaj. Shahu Maharaj said that 'Ambedkar will shine as a front-rank leader of all-India fame and appeal'. In May 1920 another All India Conference of Untouchables was held at Nagpur. Meanwhile, Ambedkar wanted to complete his study at London and hence he left India in September 1920. Despite being in London, and he was in touch with his activist friends and was monitoring the activities regularly. After returning from London, Ambedkar started socio-religious mass movement in Maharashtra. He also started a Marathi fortnightly named *Bahishkrit Bharat* on 3rd April 1927. He began to explain his views, define his aims and reply to the critics of his movement through the journal. He said that the temples and watercourses should be open to the untouchables. During these days, Bal Gangadhar Tilak was raising a slogan: *Swaraj is my birthright.* Ambedkar said that if Tilak had been born amongst the untouchables, he would have raised the slogan: *Annihilation of untouchability is my birthright.* The masses were drawn towards Ambedkar through his writings in the journal and public speeches.

After nominating as a member of Legislative Council Ambedkar made a speech in the Bombay Council on the budget on 21st February 1927 wherein he put the plight of poor farmers of India before the members. Ambedkar explained, 'How the difference in the method of levying the land revenue and the income tax worsened the lot of a poor farmer who required to pay the tax at the same rate whether he was an owner of one acre of land or a Jahagirdar or an Inamdar'. On 10th March 1927, he spoke in the Council on the prohibition policy of government, and said that the increase in the manufacture of illicit liquor in the country was entirely due to the high tariff on country liquor. Later, speaking in a separate debate, on educational system in India, he said that the government was making very slow progress in the matter of education of children.

In the third week of July 1927, Ambedkar attended a meeting at the Maangwada in Poona where he met some leaders of the Maang community. He was also in touch with the leaders of the Chamar community. On 2nd October 1927, he presided over a conference of the depressed class students in Poona. Ambedkar wanted to attract the younger and intellectual forces from the depressed classes. He also promoted the temple entry movement in Maharashtra. On 13th November 1927, in a conference of temple entry movement held at Amaravati, he said, 'The most important point we want to emphasize is not the satisfaction you get from the worship of the image of God, but the plain fact that a temple is not defiled by the presence of an untouchable, nor is the purity of the image affected by it. That is why, we oppose the idea of separate temples for us and insist on entering the existing ones'.

On 25th December 1927, a conference was organized at Mahad, a small town in Konkan Maharashtra, which is known as 'Mahad Satyagraha' or 'Chawadar Tala Satyagraha'. In this conference, Ambedkar said, 'At the outset, let me tell those, who oppose us that, we did not perish because we could not drink water from this Chawdar Tank. We now want to go to the Tank only to prove that, like others, we are also human beings'. He continued, 'This conference has been called to inaugurate an era of equality in this land'. Concluding his speech, he said, 'Hindu society should be organized on two main principles – equality and absence of casteism'. On the same day, Ambedkar burnt the *Manusmriti* and demanded a new book of law in order to reshape the Hindu code governing the life of vast of people.

On 2nd March 1930, Ambedkar launched another temple entry movement at Kalaram Temple in Nasik. The agitation continued up to the end of October 1935. The orthodox Hindus had closed the temple for a whole year. Probably, this was the longest movement in India. The agitation ended with a conference held at Yevla on 13th October 1935, where Ambedkar made a revolutionary statement: "I solemnly assure you that I will not die a Hindu". After this conference, Ambedkar did not agitate for the temple entry.

### *Round Table Conference*

Meanwhile, Ambedkar received an invitation to attend the Round Table Conference on 6th September 1930. Hence, he left Bombay for London on 4th October 1930. He declared before the conference that 'he was placing the viewpoint of one-fifth of the total population of British India – a population as large as the population of England or France – which was reduced to a position worse than that of a serf or slave'. At this conference, Ambedkar said,

> When we compare our present position with the one which it was our lot to bear in Indian society of pre-British days, we find that, instead of marching on, we are marking time. Before the British, we were in the loathsome condition due to our untouchability. Has the British Government done anything to remove it? Before the British, we could not draw water from the village well. Has the British Government secured us the right to the well? Before the British, we could not enter the temple? Can we enter now? Before the British, we were denied entry into the Police Force. Does the British Government admit us into the force? Before the British, we were not allowed to serve in the Military. Is that career now open to us? To one of these questions can we give an affirmative answer. Our wrongs have remained as open sores and they have not been righted, although 150 years of British rule have rolled away.

The most important work that Ambedkar did was the declaration of fundamental rights safeguarding the cultural, religious and economic rights of the depressed classes. He also wanted many constitutional and political safeguards to be implemented. Some of these safeguards are as below:

- The fundamental right declaring untouchability as an offence.
- Adequate representation in the legislatures through election.
- Barring a short transitional period, joint electorates with reserved seats, if universal adult franchise is

allowed; but separate electorates in the absence of universal suffrage.

- On the question of number of seats, equality in treatment based on separation of untouchables from the rest of the Hindu community and weightage to the depressed classes to compensate for their weakness in numbers as well as social, educational and economic standing.
- Before majority rule is established, emancipation of the depressed classes from the system of untouchability must be an accomplished fact. To secure this, the Constitution should declare all subjects to be equal before law and to possess equal civic rights. Any infringement on the constitutional right of equality or citizenship should be punishable under law.
- Social boycott of the depressed classes should be made punishable by law, with specific separate provisions on boycotting, like promoting a boycott or threatening a boycott. Adequate provisions should also be made to make discriminatory practices impossible in law.
- Right to adequate representation in the legislatures of the country, provincial and central, by adult suffrage and by separate electorates for the first ten years and, thereafter, by joint electorates and reserved seats.
- Adequate representation in services. As the depressed classes have suffered enormously at the hands of the high caste officers who have monopolised the public services by abusing the law or by misusing the discretion vested in them in administering them to the disadvantage of the depressed classes, the situation has to be rectified by destroying

the monopoly of the caste Hindus in the public services by regulating the recruitment in such a manner that all including the depressed classes will have an adequate share in them. For this purpose, there shall be a public service commission in each province to ensure due and adequate representation of all communities, subject to tests of efficiency in the services.

- The legislature and the executive should make adequate provision for the education, sanitation, recruitment in public services and other matters of social and political advancement of the depressed classes and to do nothing that will adversely affect them.
- The depressed classes should be given representation in the cabinets at all levels.

Besides voicing the above demands, Ambedkar gave a number of interviews and contributed articles to foreign journals. As result of this, the world came to know for the first time that the position of untouchables in India was worse than that of the Negroes in America. In the Second Round Table Conference (1931), Ambedkar strongly recommended separate electorates for the depressed castes and other minorities. Chandra and Mitra (2003) have explained some important Dalit-related issues raised by Ambedkar in the following sub-heads:

*The Chowdar Tank Protest:* At Mahad, in 1927, a conference attended by 10,000 depressed classes people was held to discuss action. It was led by Ambedkar, and the main topic of discussion was the refusal of caste Hindus to allow untouchables to take water from the communal wells even though they had the legal right to do so since 1924. It was a type of religious discrimination: Hindu allowed Christians and Muslims to draw water and it was only the presence of untouchables that offended. Ambedkar and about 10,000 delegates marched to Chowdar Tank and ceremonially exercised their civic right to use the water – probably the first march by untouchables to participate in this form of social activity for 1,000 years.

*Temple Entry Campaign:* The untouchables, 15,000 in numbers, tried to gain entry to the major temple at Nasik in order to worship Shree Rama, and sat down in front of the gates when permission was not given. An agreement between the communities led to riots and finally to closure of temple. The authors further write, 'Although the temple entry campaign did not produce sweeping reforms for untouchables, it had important effects in India and the outside world. Untouchables became extremely loyal to Ambedkar; they were increasingly driven together by common cause and a community feeling was being developed; they showed that the caste system could be successfully broken and world opinion to know about the plight of India's untouchables' (ibid.: 100).

*Ambedkar and Simon Commission:* Ambedkar became the official representative for the untouchables. When the Simon Commission came to India in 1928 to examine and report on the government system, the Congress boycotted it. Ambedkar, however, used the occasion to explain the grievances of the Dalits and suggested some ways of improving their position.

*Ambedkar and the Round Table Conference:* Ambedkar went on to represent the untouchables at the Prime Minister's Round Table Conference in London (1930). Although much of the Congress party was boycotting these conferences, most of the Indian representatives were demanding dominion status for their country. Ambedkar was not opposed to this but insisted on guarantees for untouchables as a pre-condition of self-rule. Ambedkar used the conference as an opportunity for influencing public opinion. The conference itself was inconclusive, however, although Ambedkar managed to come to an agreement with the other minority leaders for a joint stand.

The authors further write: 'The next Round Table Conference, held in 1931, turned out to be more authoritative, if only because the British authorities had expediently released from prison the leaders of the Congress party to enable them to attend. Gandhi was sympathetic to the problems of untouchables, but was completely opposed to their separation from the rest of the Hindu population. Ambedkar stood up against emotional, political and spiritual pressure of Gandhi; he refused to be dominated and stood his ground. He threw in the lot of the untouchables with the rest of the minorities, and they each agreed to recommend separate electorates for each community – much to Gandhi's disliking. This was a great achievement for Ambedkar. Up to then, the untouchables had been regarded as part of the property of the Hindu community; now they had made their case for separate treatment' (ibid.: 101).

*The Poona Pact:* The communal award in 1932 consented the depressed classes and minorities most of their requests. The Dalits were awarded two votes – one to elect their representatives to separate seats in the provincial assemblies, and the other to vote with Hindus in general constituencies. Other minorities were given separate electorates. The authors further write: 'Although Gandhi had earlier agreed to allow the British Prime Minister to arbitrate between the communities and decide the basis of representation, he now began a fast unto death protesting against the Communal Award. In the initial stage, Ambedkar showed elaborate unconcern over Gandhi's fast. Eventually, though in response to the urgent pleas of the Congress party leaders, who were fearing that Gandhi would die, he concluded an agreement with Gandhi's followers, which came to be known as the Poona Pact. More seats were reserved for the Dalits, but the candidates had to be chosen by joint electorates of both Hindus and untouchables. But, in practical terms, even though untouchables now had more representatives, they had less direct power' (ibid.: 102).

### *On the Edge of Conversion*

The agitation at Kalaram Temple, Nasik was continued till October 1935. With great efforts, great energy and great hope, Ambedkar had launched the campaign for temple entry, but the caste Hindus showed no sign of common sense and reasoning. Meanwhile, on 13th October, 1935, a conference was held at Yevla, which was attended by about 10,000 untouchables. Asking people to stop the Kalaram Temple Satyagraha, Ambedkar said, 'Unfortunately for me I was born a Hindu untouchable. It was beyond my power to prevent that. But it is within my power to refuse to live under ignoble and humiliating conditions'. Finally, he said, 'I assure you that I will not die a Hindu'. After this conference, the movement of Ambedkar turned into a new direction. After 1935, he did not go for temple entry movement as such. As soon as Ambedkar made the above statement, letters and telegrams were received by him from the leaders from the Muslim, Christian and Buddhist communities. Ambedkar was also asked to preside over different conferences held by different communities, in order to attract him towards their religion. The Muslim leader, K.L. Gouba, Bishop Brenton Thoburn Badley of Bombay and the Mahabodhi Society had contacted him. Above all, Sardar Dalip Singh Doabia from Sikh religion was also in touch with him. But, Ambedkar was not in a hurry. He wanted to discuss the issue of conversion at a Mahar conference though it was discussed at different conferences and with a number of people. But Ambedkar did not declare the religion to which he was converting.

A conference of the Mahars was held at Dadar, Bombay on 30th and 31st May 1936. The conference was important since it had a background of Yevla conference. The conference was attended by Christian, Sikh and Muslim leaders and priests. Since other segments of the untouchables were differed on the issue of conversion, Ambedkar called a conference of only Mahars. He was of the opinion that the untouchables must go out of the Hindu fold to secure true freedom for their activities such as wearing dress, eating food, securing jobs, receiving education and living in the midst of a civilized society. Further, he stated to his people that, 'Because of untouchability, your merits go unrewarded; there is no appreciation of your mental and physical qualities'. The conference was concluded with a resolution that the Mahar community was prepared to change a religion and to stop visiting the Hindu places of worship. In the next phase, Ambedkar had talks with a number of religious leaders. He studied all the religions and, finally, he decided to embrace Buddhism. On 14th October 1956, Ambedkar along with his five lakh followers embraced Buddhism. After 1956, Ambedkar could establish a new identity as Buddhist for the untouchables of India. The new religion of untouchables, i.e., Buddhism, talks about the freedom and equality, which is contrary to Hinduism. The Mahars of Maharashtra have been maintaining this identity till now.

### *Political Success and Representation of Labour Class*

The provincial autonomy under the Government of India Act, 1935 was carried out in 1937, hence, the coming election was important for all political parties. Ambedkar founded a new political party named, Independent Labour Party, in August 1936. The party was focusing on the needs and grievances of the landless, poor tenants and workers. Ambedkar launched an election campaign. He mainly concentrated on Bombay province. He toured all the districts of Maharashtra and delivered speeches at Nasik, Ahmednagar, Solapur, Satara, Belgaum, etc. The election took place on February 17, 1937. Ambedkar and his party secured a big success in this election. Out of 17 candidates, put by the party, 15 were elected. Ambedkar himself was elected with a huge margin. During his stint at assembly, he introduced a number of bills like, Bill to Abolish Khoti System, Bill to Abolish the Mahar Vatan, etc. He also spoke on different issues. Ambedkar was the first legislator in India to introduce a bill for the abolition of the serfdom of agricultural tenants.

On 13th May 1938, Ambedkar went on a tour of Konkan Maharashtra and addressed several meetings and rallies organized by the tenants and agricultural labourers. The bill for the abolition of the khoti system introduced by Ambedkar was postponed for ten years by the Congress. But, Ambedkar continued to fight for this issue. He took this issue to the masses. In September 1938, Industrial Disputes Bill was brought to the assembly. Ambedkar opposed this saying that it declares the strike as illegal, whereas this must be a right of workers. On another occasion, Ambedkar called a strike of workers of Bombay and it was the first successful strike launched against a popular government. On 6th January 1939, Ambedkar addressed a large gathering of agriculturists at Mahad. He explained the negative attitude of Congress government towards agriculturists. Thus, Ambedkar could also able to establish his leadership among the agriculturists and industrial workers. He represented, in a real sense, the labour class in the assembly with commitment.

Ambedkar founded the All India Scheduled Castes Federation, a political organization, in 1942. The organization was representing the Scheduled Castes (SCs). In 1945, elections were held and the organization failed to win even a single seat. This was very sad experience for it and Ambedkar as well. It was something, he was to later experience again, for the record of Ambedkar's last few years was that of a fruitless campaign for proper political representation for Dalits.

### *Framer of the Indian Constitution*

The talks on the independence was carried out constructively by the Viceroy in June 1947. Ambedkar was a member of the Flag Committee of the Constituent Assembly. On 22nd July 1947, the Constituent Assembly adopted the tri-colour flag with Ashoka Chakra on it as the National Flag. Earlier, in a meeting with Ambedkar over the flag, some of the leaders suggested to have Charakha. Later, they were disappointed by seeing the Ashoka Chakra, instead of Charakha. This was a rational decision taken by Ambedkar. The British Parliament passed the Act of Indian Independence on 15th July 1947. In the last week of July 1947 the names of the ministers for the first cabinet of free India were discussed. Ambedkar was included as the Law Minister of free India. India got its independence on 15th August 1947. On 29th

August 1947, the Constituent Assembly appointed a drafting committee of seven members and Ambedkar was appointed as its chairman. Ambedkar worked hard to frame the Indian Constitution. The Constitution, which had to govern the people, was the most important document. He is also called the chief architect of the Constitution of India. This can be seen from a speech of T.T. Krishnamachari made on 5th November 1948 in the Constituent Assembly. He said, 'The House is perhaps aware that of the seven members nominated. One had resigned from the House and was replaced. One died and was not replaced. One was away in America and his place was not filled up and another person was engaged in state affairs and there was void to that extent. One or two people were far away from Delhi and perhaps reasons of health did not permit them to attend. So it happened ultimately that the entire burden of drafting the Constitution fell on Ambedkar and I have no doubt that we are grateful to him for having achieved this task in a manner which is undoubtedly commendable'.

In the last week of February 1948, Ambedkar completed the drafting of Constitution and submitted it to the Constituent Assembly. The Draft Constitution contained 315 articles and eight schedules. The Constitution is more important so far as the weaker sections of Indian society, such as SCs, STs and OBCs, are concerned. It has protected them by certain privileges. Some of the important articles and their contents are as below:

| | |
|---|---|
| Article 14 | Equality before law. |
| Article 15 | Prohibition of discrimination on grounds of religion, race, caste, sex, place of birth or any of them. |
| Article 16 | Equal opportunities in matters of employment. |
| Article 17 | Untouchability as a punishable offence. |

| | |
|---|---|
| Article 19 | Freedom of speech. |
| Article 23 | The trafficking in human beings, begging and forced labour made punishable offences. |
| Article 24 | Protection of children from child labour. |
| Article 45 | Free and compulsory education for all children. |
| Article 46 | Promoting the educational and economic interests of the weaker sections such as SCs and STs. |
| Articles 143, | 330, 332, 334, etc., Explain the reservation for SCs and STs in different authorities of the government. |

There are also a number of articles which govern the interests of the majority people. It protects the Bahujans from all types of social, economic and political injustice. It, thus, gives freedom and equality to all the segments of the society. The framing of India's Constitution has been one of the major achievements of Ambedkar.

## Revival of Buddhism by Ambedkar

In the last phase of the life of Babasaheb Ambedkar, a revolutionary incident took place, which was a big blow to the Hindu society. This was a beginning of the intellectual war. Ambedkar wanted to revive Buddhism in India. In this effort, he attended a number of conferences, which were mainly devoted to Buddhism. He was also thinking of writing a book on Buddhism. As stated earlier, long before in 1935 at Yevla, he had declared that, 'Though I born a Hindu, I do not intend to die a Hindu'. In the month of December 1954, Ambedkar attended the third Buddhist World Conference at Rangoon. At that time the state of his health was critical. He also attended conferences on Buddhism in Sri Lanka (1950), Burma (now Myanmar) (1954) and Nepal

(1956). In Nepal, he delivered a lecture on 'Buddhism and Communism', in which he stated that Buddhism is superior and different than Communism. Despite his ill-health, Ambedkar wrote an important book titled as *The Buddha and His Dhamma* – a product of great research. In May 1956, his talk on Buddhism was broadcasted by BBC, London in which Ambedkar said, 'I prefer Buddhism because it gives three principles in combination, which no other religion does. Buddhism teaches *Prajna* (understanding as against superstition and supernaturalism), *Karuna* (love) and *Samata* (equality). This is what man wants for a good and happy life. Neither God nor soul can save society'.

According to Ambedkar, Buddhism differs from Hinduism. He said, 'Hinduism believes in God. Buddhism has no God. Hinduism believes in soul. According to Buddhism, there is no soul. Hinduism believes in Chaturvarna and the caste system. Buddhism has no place for the caste system and Chaturvarna'.

In 1954, Ambedkar established the Buddhist Society of India, which was registered on May 4, 1956. He was the chairman of this Society. Its main objective was to spread the Buddhism in India, especially in Maharashtra. Unfortunately, Ambedkar died on December 6, 1956, within a short period of its formation, and thus, the Society lost its visionary chairman. However, Yashavant Ambedkar, the son of B.R. Ambedkar, was entrusted with the responsibility. After the death of Yashavant, it went to Meeratai Ambedkar, the daughter-in-law of Ambedkar. It may be pertinent to mention that the Society has been involved in a number of camps, meets, conferences for the spread of Buddhism. It also has been publishing books on Buddhism to guide the followers.

On 24th May 1956, on the day of Buddha Jayanti, at Nare Park, Bombay, Ambedkar declared that he would embrace Buddhism in October 1956. On 23rd September 1956, he issued a press note announcing that his conversion to Buddhism would take place at Nagpur on 14th October 1956. After the declaration of the day for conversion, the arrangements were carried out at Nagpur. The followers of Ambedkar were also preparing and waiting for this occasion. For a week prior to this day, thousands of men, women and children of the depressed castes, especially the Mahars, began pouring into Nagpur from Marathi-speaking areas of Central Provinces and Bombay. They were shouting the slogans like "Bhagwan Buddha ki Jay", "Babasaheb ki Jay", etc. An open ground of 14 acres near the Vaccine Institute at Shraddhanand Peth, Nagpur, was booked as the venue for embracing Buddhism (the place is known as *Diksha Bhoomi*). Two special large pandals were created, one for men and the other for women. Buddhist flags consisting of blue, red and green stripes fluttered everywhere. All the surrounding places were decorated. On the evening of 13th October 1956, Ambedkar held a press conference and declared that his Buddhism would be called as neo-Buddhism or 'Navayana'. Further, he stated that, 'Buddhism is a part and parcel of *Bharatiya* culture. I have taken care that, my conversion will not harm the tradition of the culture and history of this land". He predicted that, "in the next ten or fifteen years, the wave of mass conversion would spread all over the country, and India would become a Buddhist country. Brahmins would be the last to follow and let them be the last'.

On 14th October 1956, Ambedkar reached the *Deeksha Bhoomi* in white silk dhoti and white coat, along with his wife Savita Ambedkar. On the dias, along with Ambedkar, D. Valisinha, Ven. M. Sanghratna Thera, Ven. H. Sadda Tissa Thera and Ven. Pannanand Thera were present. Millions of followers of Ambedkar had congregated. The 83-year-old Mahasthaver Chandramani of Kushinara administered the ceremony. The three *Saranas* (under Buddha, Dhamma and Sangha) and *Panchasheel* (five precepts of abstention from killing, stealing, telling lies, wrongful sexual life, and drink) were vowed. Then, they bowed down thrice with clasped hands before the Buddha statue. Thus, Ambedkar embraced Buddhism. At this moment, Ambedkar declared that, 'By discarding my ancient religion which stood for inequality and oppression, today I am reborn. I have no faith in the philosophy of incarnation, it is wrong and mischievous to say that Buddha was an incarnation of Vishnu. I am no more a devotee of any Hindu god or goddess. I will not perform *shraddha*. I will strictly follow the eightfold path of Buddha. Buddhism is a true religion and I will lead a life guided by the three principles of knowledge, right path and compassion'. After embracing Buddhism, Ambedkar administered the ceremony for his followers. Nearly three lakhs of his followers embraced Buddhism. They were shouting slogans as, "Bhagwan Buddha ki Jay" and "Babasaheb ki Jay".

The next day, Ambedkar gave a speech to his followers at the same place. He said that the Scheduled Castes (SCs) would not lose their rights by embracing Buddhism. He also reminded his vow taken in 1935 at Yevla. He further stated, 'Man cannot live by bread alone. He has a mind, which needs for thought. Religion instills hope in man and drives him to activity. Hindu religion has watered down the enthusiasm of the down-trodden. And I found it necessary to change my faith and embrace Buddhism'. Ambedkar explained his followers, how Hinduism was treating the untouchables and what would be the position of untouchables in Buddhism.

The 14th of October, the day of embracing the Buddhism by Ambedkar and his followers, is known as *Dhammachakra Pravartana Din.* On this day, every year, lakhs of people from India, especially from Maharashtra, arrive at *Diksha Bhoomi,* Nagpur, to pay a tribute to Ambedkar and also to embrace Buddhism. As a result of Ambedkar's revolutionary decision, his followers, especially, the Mahars of Maharashtra, have accepted Buddhism as their religion. They have also developed their own culture under Buddhism. The two important organizations, dedicated to the spread of Buddhism, have been working in India. The first is called the Buddhist Society of India (established by Babasaheb Ambedkar) and Trilokya Mahasangh. Besides these, there are several local and regional level bodies, which are working for spread of Buddhism. In India, all the followers believe in Ambedkar's Buddhism. Every social or public ceremony is addressed by garlanding and paying tribute to two most important persons, viz., Tathagat Bhagwan Goutam Buddha and Bharatratna Babasaheb Ambedkar. Every Buddhist follows this tradition.

Naik (2003: 44) describes the post-conversion situation in Maharashtra in a different manner. According to him, 'The number of atrocities inflicted on the untouchables outdo the instances of conversion by the differences of 36 cases in Maharashtra during the period between 1956 and 1964. As a result, there were more and more instances of untouchable converts to Buddhism and more and more number of atrocities inflicted on them. Thus, more the conversions, more the atrocities'. Valisinha, the General Secretary of Mahabodhi Society of India, has pointed out that, 'The upsurge of Buddhism in India is the most remarkable event of the present century. It is unprecedented. No one imagined such a thing possible in the twentieth century. The credit for this remarkable achievement in history goes to Dr Bhimrao Ambedkar' (cited in Grover, 1993: 272). Ambedkar was trying to hold a number of mass conversions. Some of them took place in the presence of Ambedkar. But, unfortunately, the process of mass conversions could not continue for long. On 6th December 1956, i.e., after one and half month of conversion ceremony, Babasaheb Ambedkar's life came to an end. This was a big blow for the mission of spreading Buddhism in India.

In the contemporary period, all the Mahars follow the Buddhist culture, contrary to Hindu culture. Some of them have embraced Buddhism and some of them have not embraced, but follow. There is an insignificant size of population, which adheres to Hindu culture. However, Ambedkar has given a revolutionary turn to Buddhism, which is followed by every follower. It is believed that the real Ambedkarites are those, who follow the Ambedkarism along with Buddhism. This could be seen in India, especially in Maharashtra.

### The Last of Journey

After the revolutionary conversion ceremony held at Nagpur, Ambedkar went to Delhi. He wanted to arrange the conversion ceremonies in Delhi, Uttar Pradesh, Punjab and Bombay too. Those days, Ambedkar was ailing seriously. His eyesight was also poor. He was worried about the spread of Buddhism in India. He wanted to modify the outlook of the

Sangha. He said that, 'the Bhikkus should become like the Christian missionaries, social workers and social preachers'. Despite his serious health, Ambedkar attended the World Buddhist Conference held at Kathmandu, Nepal, during 15th–20th November 1956. The conference was inaugurated by the King Mahendra of Nepal in the Sangha Darbar Gallery Hall. Ambedkar was requested to speak on 'Ahimsa in Buddhism'. But, on the last minutes, majority of the delegates pressed him to speak on 'Buddha and Karl Marx'. Ambedkar accepted and delivered a remarkable speech, which is known as 'Buddhism and Communism'. He explained how the Buddhism is different from communism and how Buddha was superior to Marx. He said that the Buddhist system was a democratic system whereas the communist system was based on dictatorship. He also expressed how Buddhism was for the humanity. On his way back, he also gave speeches at Benaras Hindu University and Kashi Vidyapeeth. On 30th November 1956, he returned to Delhi. He was ill, sad, worried and depressed. The last journey of Ambedkar started from the beginning of December 1956. His last six days passed as below:

*1st December, 1956:* In the evening, Ambedkar visited an exhibition held at Mathura Road, Delhi. The exhibition was about the Buddhist art. He saw the exhibition with great interest. On his way back to home, he also visited a bookshop at Connaught Place, Delhi. He saw the new arrivals and placed the order for some select books.

*2nd December, 1956:* Ambedkar attended a function held at Ashok Vihar, Delhi, in honour of the Dalai Lama, who had come to India to attend the winter celebration of the 2,500th Buddha Jayanti to be held at Bodh Gaya. In the evening, he discussed some issues with his devotees at his residence.

*3rd December, 1956:* In the evening, Ambedkar asked his attendants to keep chairs on the lawns. He was tired. At this moment, a group photograph was taken by Mrs Ambedkar's brother (Balu Kabir). The photograph includes Ambedkar, Mrs Ambedkar, K.V. Kabir (Mrs Ambedkar's father) and Dr Malvankar. In the night, Ambedkar went (with the help of Rattu) to inquire the health of Mali (the gardener), who had been ill for over three days.

*4th December, 1956:* In the morning, Ambedkar asked Rattu to make enquiries at the Railway Booking Office of Delhi about the reservation of tickets for 14th December 1956. On 16th December 1956, a programme of conversion was to be held at Bombay and Ambedkar wanted to attend that. Ambedkar was also present in the Council of States and had a discussion. In the evening, he dictated two important letters, one to P.K. Atre, and the other to S.M. Joshi (both were front-ranking leaders in Samyukta Maharashtra) about the proposed Republican Party. Although Ambedkar and his associates were supposed to leave Delhi for Bombay on 14th December 1956, the schedule was changed. On 4th December, Mrs Ambedkar's father and her brother left Delhi by the evening train for Bombay. Now, Ambedkar was left with Mrs Ambedkar, Dr Malvankar and Rattu.

*5th December, 1956:* In the early morning, Rattu, the attendant, saw that Ambedkar was sleeping. In the afternoon, Mrs Ambedkar left home with Dr Malvankar for shopping. Ambedkar enquired about his wife thrice, but she had not returned. Ambedkar was terribly upset. Mrs Ambedkar returned with Dr Malvanakar at 5.30 in the evening. Ambedkar was in an angry mood. In the night, at 8 p.m., a delegation of the Jain leaders came to meet him. The Jain leaders were requesting Ambedkar to attend a function, the next morning and discuss some points with their Muni. He agreed, if his health permitted. The Jain leaders were the last visitors of Ambedkar. While Ambedkar was talking to the Jain leaders, Dr Malvankar, the guest, also left his place and went to Bombay by the night plane. He was the last guest.

In the night, Rattu was massaging Ambedkar's legs. Ambedkar was singing Buddham Saranam Gachchami. Then, he went for dinner. He ate little. Rattu massaged on head. He went to bedroom with books. After having a look on the books, at around 11 p.m., Ambedkar went to sleep. Rattu took leave from his master and left for his home. As soon as he passed the gate, Ambedkar called him again and asked to bring the typescripts of the preface and the introduction to *The Buddha and His Dhamma* and the typed letters to P.K. Atre and S.M. Joshi. Ambedkar wanted to re-look at these papers. He went through them in the late night and slept.

*6th December, 1956:* At about 6.30 a.m., Mrs Ambedkar got up and had a look at the bed of Ambedkar. Ambedkar was in deep sleep and his leg was resting on a cushion. She came inside and tried to wake up Ambedkar. But Ambedkar was no more. He had been departed from this world. He had passed away in sleep.

The place where Ambedkar was passed away was 26, Alipore Road, Delhi. All the admirers and devotees of Ambedkar gathered at this place. Jawaharlal Nehru, Jagjivan Ram, the secretaries of the Lok Sabha and the Rajya Sabha and several Members of Parliament, leading lawyers and eminent scholars paid their homage to the great leader, Babasaheb Ambedkar. The body was brought to Bombay by plane. The plane took off at 9.30 p.m. from Delhi and reached Bombay at 3 a.m. on 7th December 1956. Bhiku Anand Kousalyayan, Mrs Ambedkar, Rattu and a few others accompanied his body. The body was brought to 'Rajgriha' at Dadar, Bombay. Several political leaders, trade union leaders and lakhs of people had gathered there. All the factories, docks, railway workshops, textile mills, schools, colleges and cinemas were closed in Bombay. At about 1.30 p.m., the funeral procession started from Vincent Road (later renamed as Babasaheb Ambedkar Road), and passed through Poibavdi, Elphinstone Bridge, Sayani Road and Gokhale Road, for the Dadar Hindu Crematorium. The procession reached the crematorium at around 5.30 p.m., after four hours' journey. More than 5 lakhs of people were present. About one lakh people embraced Buddhism at the crematorium, as a honour to their great leader. S.L. Silam, Mrs Savita Ambedkar, B.S. Gaikwad, R.D. Bhandare, B.C. Kamble, P.T. Kamble, M.V. Donde, P.K. Atre and other eminent persons were present. The death of Ambedkar was a big shock to the untouchables. They had lost their leader. The movement of untouchables or Scheduled Castes was now without their scholar leader.

The place, where Ambedkar was cremated, has been known as *Chaityabhoomi*. A small piece of land was given by the Government of Maharashtra, where a stupa was constructed. On 6th December, every year, i.e., on the occasion of death anniversary of Ambedkar or on the occasion of Mahaparinirvana of Ambedkar, lakhs of people from all over India, especially Maharashtra, visit the Chaityabhoomi to pay a tribute to their departed leader. The day has become most important in the life of Ambedkar's followers.

### Summary

Babasaheb Ambedkar was a multidimensional person. His contribution to the Indian society has been remarkable. With the background of an untouchable, he achieved the highest score in the educational field. He obtained a number of degrees from foreign universities. After coming to India, he served for the society. He spent his whole life for the development of untouchables. He conducted various conferences and meets, where he opposed the Hindu caste system. He fought for the equality and freedom. He represented the labour classes like agriculturists and industrial workers too. Through the Constitution, he made provisions for the development of SCs, STs and OBCs. Hence, Ambedkar not only represented the untouchables, but also others. He gave a new way of life to the untouchables in the form of Buddhism. This was a new religion as against Hinduism. The untouchables, especially the Mahars, have embraced Buddhism in a big number and have been practising it. The untouchables and the neo-Buddhists of India have not forgotten Ambedkar and his socio-political activities. All the private and public celebrations of the Mahars or neo-Buddhists have been carried out by paying a tribute to two personalities: one is, Tathagat Goutam Buddha and the other is, Babasaheb Ambedkar. On the occasion of the birth anniversary of Ambedkar (i.e., 14th April), number of programmes are celebrated at rural and urban locations in Maharashtra. On the occasion of Dhamma Chakra Pravartana Din (i.e., 14th October), lakhs of people visit the Diksha Bhoomi, Nagpur and on the occasion of death anniversary of Ambedkar (i.e., 6th December), lakhs of his followers visit the Chaityabhoomi, Mumbai. This shows the love and spirit of the masses for Ambedkar. No doubt, Ambedkar was a remarkable mass leader of India.

## References

Chandra, Ramesh and Sangh Mittra (2003), *The Ambedkar Era*, Commonwealth Publishers, New Delhi.

Grover, Virender (Ed.)(1993), *B.R. Ambedkar: Political Thinker of Modern India*, Deep and Deep Publication, New Delhi.

Keer, Dhananjay (1954, reprinted, 1971), *Ambedkar: Life and Mission*, Popular Prakashan, Bombay.

Moon, Vasant (Ed.), *Baba Saheb Ambedkar: Writings & Speeches*, Vol. 2, Government of Maharashtra Publication.

Naik, C.D. (2003), *Thoughts and Philosophy of Dr B.R. Ambedkar*, Sarup and Sons, New Delhi.

The Buddhist Society of India (2004), *Bouddhanchi Pavitra Sthale*, a booklet, published by the Buddhist Society of India.

# Chapter 2

# Ambedkar's Thoughts on Agriculture and Their Relevance

## With Respect to Small Holdings

The thoughts of Ambedkar on social and political views have been interpreted and reinterpreted by various scholars. But, Ambedkar's thoughts on economics are not as widely known. The contribution of Ambedkar to the field of economics is remarkable. His basic research was in economics. His Ph.D. research explains his views on public finance. He also did his research for D.Sc. on 'The Problems of the Rupee: Its Origin and its Solution'. Thus, his major research was in economics. He focused on money, public finance, trade, exchange rate, etc. Above all, Ambedkar also contributed much to agricultural economics, which is often neglected. Ambedkar can be acknowledged as the father of 'land reforms'. The foundation of land reforms in India, which was brought out by the Government of India after independence, was laid long back in 1937. He had also expressed his views on the small holdings, collective farming, khoti system, private moneylenders, etc. His arguments were so potent that the relevance of these thoughts can be found even in the contemporary period.

## Ambedkar's Thoughts on Small Holdings

Discussing Ambedkar's contribution to agricultural economics, especially to Indian agriculture, would be large enough a subject, hence, we propose to consider only one aspect of his thoughts. We select his thoughts on small holdings.

An article of Babasaheb Ambedkar was published in the *Journal of the Indian Economic Society (Babasaheb Ambedkar: Writings and Speeches,* Vol. I, 1918), titled 'Small Holdings in India and their Remedies'. Ambedkar had analysed the problems of small holdings in Indian agriculture long back in 1918. Similar kind of problems can be seen even in the contemporary period. He also had given a solution for this problem, which was a major part of land reforms of India, declared in the post-independent India.

Ambedkar has discussed this topic in five parts. The importance of agriculture has been explained in the first part. The second part deals with the main content, i.e., small holdings in India. The third and the fourth parts talk about consolidation and enlargement, respectively. In the last part, Ambedkar has given the remedies for it.

Ambedkar has juxtaposed the extent of large holdings with respect to England and the small holdings with respect to India. He has concentrated on India's position for studying the small holdings. He has thrown light on average size of holdings in different provinces of India (where he referred to Report of the Committee, Baroda State, 1917) and a village named Pimpala Soudagar near Pune (where he referred to land and labour in a Deccan village). Ambedkar has shown that, 'the average size of holdings varies from 25.9 acres in the Bombay presidency to an acre or two in Pimpala Soudagar'. He further stated that, 'this diminutive size of holding is said to be greatly harmful to Indian agriculture.

The evils of small holdings are many'. The average size of agricultural holding in India after 1950–51 has been declining, which has generated serious problems. The average size of an operation holding in India has been falling from 3.12 hectare in 1953–54 to 2.62 hectare in 1960–61, 2.30 hectare in 1970–71, 2 hectare in 1976–77, 1.80 hectare in 1980 and 1.68 hectare in 1985. Finally, it came down to 1.5 hectare in 1995–96 (Agricultural Census, 2000). Ambedkar has linked the small holdings with the agricultural productivity. The smaller the holding, lower would be the productivity. Even in the current period, similar trend can be found in India. A number of studies have been done in the post-1950s, which have pointed to the same observation. In this regard, Amartya Sen (1962) has stated that 'productivity per acre decreased with the size of holding'. G.G. Saini (1979) also has established the same point. He says that, 'by and large, inverse relationship between farm size and productivity is a confirmed phenomenon in Indian agriculture'. The western economists like Cohen (1956), Thomas (1960) and others also have suggested a similar kind of relationship which Ambedkar had proposed long back. Yet, none of the syllabus on economics of agriculture in Indian universities, has focused on Ambedkar's contribution. The relevance of the relationship built by Ambedkar can be found even in the twenty-first century. The average size of agricultural landholding has been declining even in the recent period and as a result of that, the productivity also has declined. This fact supports Ambedkar's argument.

Ambedkar also has thrown a clear light on the concept of economic holding. He has referred to Keatinge (*Rural Economy in the Bombay Deccan*, p. 51). Keatinge has defined an economic holding as, 'a holding which allows a man chance of producing sufficient grain to support himself and his family in reasonable comfort, after paying his necessary expenses' (quoted in *Babasaheb Ambedkar: Writings and Speeches*, Vol. 1, p. 466). He also has referred to writings of Prof. Jevons, whose view on the economic holding is from the standpoint of consumption rather than of production. Ambedkar differed with them and has given a different version. He stated that, 'On the definition of an economic holding, we can postulate that, if agriculture is to be treated as an economic enterprise, then, by itself, there could be no such thing as a large or a small holding. To a farmer a holding is too small or too large for the factors of production at his disposal necessary for carrying on the cultivation of his holding as an economic enterprise. Mere size of land is empty of all economic connotations. Consequently, it cannot possibly be the language of economic science to say that, a large holding is economic, while a small holding is uneconomic. It is the right or wrong proportion of other factors of production to a unit that renders the latter economic farm; for, economic or uneconomic does not depend upon the size of land but upon the due proportion among all the factors including land' (ibid.).

Ambedkar gave a production-based meaning to economic holding. Any size of land could be stated as economic, provided that, it could arrange proper combination of inputs. Ambedkar said that, 'An economic holding consists of a combination of land, capital and labour, etc., in proportion such that the contribution of each in conjunction with the rest is the highest. The farmers must have the other instruments of production required for the efficient cultivation of his holding' (ibid.). Thus, Ambedkar has given a strong base to the meaning of economic holding, that is, if there are proper arrangements of soil, technology, efficient labour, crops, etc., then it could make the land viable in the economic sense. All the contemporary authors, who have described the economic holding and its effects, go strictly according to Ambedkar's argument. The Congress Agrarian Reforms Committee (1949) has defined an economic holding as one, which could provide a reasonable standard of living to the cultivator and give full employment for a family of normal size. Although the wording of the definition differs, but it goes on the line of Ambedkar. Any size of land could give a good standard of living and proper employment, if it arranges all required inputs in the most efficient way. The Central Panel on Land Reforms has fixed the size of economic holding on the basis of average income earned from that holding. According to that, 'a farm which yields an average income of Rs 1,600, excluding remuneration for family labour, per annum may be considered as economic holding' (Sadhu and Singh, 1998: 202). On these bases, some of the scholars have fixed the size of land as 2 acres. Besides these, Ambedkar's view on economic holding seems to be clear. Because, unless the farmer manages the required proper inputs including land, labour and capital, even 2 acres or Rs 1,600 could not give a good standard of life. If a farmer follows efficient combination of inputs, as told by Ambedkar, he may be earning five times of the fixed income or he may be enjoying a better standard of living. Hence, the mere size of the land is not important, but other required inputs are also equally important. Ambedkar had realized the importance of capital and capital goods in 1918, which can be traced to the history of Indian agriculture of the post-independence period. Ambedkar says that, 'Consequently the remedy for the ills of agriculture in India does not lie primarily in the matter of enlarging holdings but in the matter of increasing capital and capital goods' (*Babasaheb Ambedkar: Writings and Speeches*, Vol. 1, p. 472). The Green Revolution, which has been stated as a landmark in the agricultural history, was a result of combination of efficient factors of production and use of capital goods. In the contemporary period, a number of agricultural universities and other scholars have also been emphasizing on the efficient arrangement of land, labour and capital. The Government of India also has been focusing on the process of mechanization, as a part of capital goods, in Indian agriculture. In every Five-Year Plan, there has been a focus on the mechanization. However, from the Sixth Plan, selective mechanization in Indian agriculture has been promoted. Therefore, it can be stated that the views of Ambedkar on economic holdings are relevant even in the contemporary period of time.

Ambedkar also has thrown light on idle labour. According to him, 'A large agricultural population with the lowest proportion of land in actual cultivation means that a large part of the agricultural population is superfluous and idle' (ibid.). He further said that, 'the economic effects of this idle labour is that it adds to the tremendous amount of pressure that our agricultural population exerts on land' (ibid.). In other words, according to Ambedkar, the idle labour is unproductive. Similar kind of explanation has been given by the famous economist, Nurkse Ragnar in 1953, in agricultural economics. Nurkse has used the terminology, the disguised unemployment instead of idle labour. But, Ambedkar had already propounded similar theory long back in 1918, which was 35 years before Nurkse. Idle labour has been the most common problem in Indian agriculture, even in the twenty-first century. The dependency rate over agriculture in 2001 was 64 per cent (Tenth Five-Year Plan Proceedings: 2002–07), which shows that there has been tremendous pressure on agricultural land. Hence, it can be stated that, Ambedkar's views in this regard also seem to be true even in the contemporary time.

Ambedkar also has given the reasons for the division of land in India. According to him, 'Notwithstanding what others have said, this enormous pressure is the chief cause of the subdivision of land. It is the failure to grasp the working of this pressure on land that makes the law of inheritance such a great grievance. To say that, the law of inheritance causes subdivision of land is to give a false view by inverting the real situation. The mere existence of the law cannot be complained of as a grievance. The grievance consists in the fact that, it is invoked. But why is it invoked even when it is injurious? Simply, because it is profitable. There is nothing strange in this. When farming is the only occupation, to get a small piece of land is better than to have none. Thus the grievance lies in the circumstances which put a premium on these small pieces of land. The premium, is no doubt, due to the large population depending solely on agriculture to eke out its living. Naturally, a population that has little else to prefer to agriculture will try to invoke every possible cause to get a piece of land however small. It is therefore, the law of inheritance that is the evil, but it is the high pressure on land, which brings it into operation. People cultivate the small piece not because their standard of living is low, but it the only profitable thing for them to do at present. If they had something more profitable to do, they would never prefer the small piece' (*Babasaheb Ambedkar: Writings and Speeches*, Vol. 1, p. 474). Thus, Ambedkar explained the most important economic reason for the division of land, which could be stated as one of the most important cause for the division of agricultural land in India.

In the end, Ambedkar also has suggested important remedies for the problems of Indian agriculture, especially regarding the subdivision and fragmentation of land. According to him, 'The remedy for preventing subdivision and fragmentation of consolidated holdings cannot be expected to bring real relief. Instead, it will only serve to be legal eyewash' (ibid.). Further, he argued that, 'even if we enlarged the existing holdings and procured capital goods to make them economic, we will not only be not advocating the proper remedy but will end in aggravating the evils' (ibid.). Finally, Ambedkar has strongly recommended the industrialization in India. He argued that, 'Industrialiszation of India is the soundest remedy for the agricultural problems of India. The cumulative effects of industrialiszation, namely, a lessening pressure and an increasing amount of capital and capital goods will forcibly create the economic necessity of enlarging the holding' (ibid.). This was nothing but a positive relationship between the agricultural and industrial sectors. In the post-independence period, the Government of India has been following a similar policy. The government has promoted the industries, especially agro-based industries. The agro-based industries have transmitted an industrial culture in rural areas and have promoted modernization and innovation in agriculture. The ultimate result of all this is the development of Indian agriculture.

## Conclusion

Thus, Babasaheb Ambedkar has offered remarkable insights into the small holdings of India. Surprisingly, the views expressed in 1918, can be applied even in the present time. The relevance of Ambedkar's views cannot be doubted. He has explained his views on economic holdings, idle labour, reasons for division of land, remedies for the agricultural problems, etc. The relationship built by or the explanation given by Ambedkar has been repeated by many Indian as well as western economists. But, no scholar has paid any attention to the original work of Ambedkar. Theories in agricultural economics have sought to explain the relationship between the agriculture and industrial sector (for example, Lewis, 1964 and Ranis-Fei, 1967). Hence, it can be stated that these theories have a link with Ambedkar's theory. More important is that the relevance of Ambedkar's views on small holdings has been a central part of the agricultural history of Indian agriculture. The Government of India has been promoting the agriculture and industry, which are interdependent. The relevance of Ambedkar's theory can be found in each of the Five-Year Plans, which has been promoting the agricultural sector. The Government of India had announced a National Agricultural Policy on 28th July 2000 to face the challenges of globalization. Some of the sub-policies are: 'Progressive Institutionalization of Rural and Farm Credit', 'Encouraging Private Investment in Agriculture' and 'Encouraging Agri-research, Human Resource Development, Management, Marketing, Rural Electrification, etc.' (*Economic Survey*: 2000–2001). These policies are nothing but application of Ambedkar's thoughts on agriculture. Ambedkar had recommended the use of capital and capital goods. The Government of India has been promoting these requirements in the phase of globalization. Even after 87 years of Ambedkar's formulation of his theory, it remains equally viable.

## References

*Ambedkar Babasaheb: Writings and Speeches*, Compiled by Vasant Moon, Vol.1, Education Department, Government of Maharashtra Publication, p. 457.

Agricultural Census (2000), Government of India publication.

Cohen, R.L. (1956), *The Economics of Agriculture*, Cambridge University Press, London.

Economic Survey 2000–2001, Government of India Publication.

Nurkse, Ragnar (1953), *Problems of Capital Formation in Underdeveloped Countries*, Oxford University Press, London.

Sadhu, A.N. and Amarjit Singh (1998), *Fundamentals of Agricultural Economics*, Himalaya Publishing House, New Delhi, p. 202.

Saini, G. G. (1979), *Farm Size, Resource Use, Efficiency and Income Distribution* Allied Publication, New Delhi.

Sen, Amartya (1964),. Size of Holdings and Productivity, *Economic & Political Weekly*, Vol. 16, February, 1964. [also see, Sen Amartya (1964), "An Aspect of Indian Agriculture", *Economic & Political Weekly*, Vol. 4, Feb.1964.]

Tenth Five-Year Plan: Proceedings (2002–2007).

Thomas, Edgar (1960), *An Introduction to Agricultural Economics*, Nelson Press, New York.

Zutshi, Ravi (1994), "Enhancing India's Competitive Position through Agro-industrial Development", *Indian Journal of Public Administration*, Vol. XL, No. 2, April–June, 1994.

# Chapter 3

# Ambedkar's Thoughts on Inclusive Policies in Indian Agriculture

Exclusion and inclusion are multidimensional processes in society. These are always expressed against a social background. Some forces in the society play a dominant role and create the exclusion process. The process of exclusion can be analysed with reference to caste, religion, gender, class, education, economics, politics, etc. In the most simple words, exclusion is nothing but an alienation of certain people or community within the society. Lynn Todman (2004) argued that, 'the social exclusion refers to the processes in which individuals and entire community of people are systematically blocked from the rights, opportunities and resources, which are normally available to the society'. The process of exclusion creates social and economic inequality. An inequality in the society can lead to the social and cultural conflicts. Therefore, in order to strike a balance within the society, the process of inclusion needs to be promoted.

Social inclusion is a strategy to fight against the demerits of exclusion existing in the society. The process of inclusion promotes equality and discourages inequality. The social inclusion strategy can be framed as per the type and degree of exclusion. The social exclusion in

India is based on the caste system, which has created the highest degree of social and economic inequality. This inequality has continued for years and ages. Ambedkar fought against social exclusion and promoted the process of inclusion. As a result, the Government of India too adopted a number of inclusive policies for the development of backward castes.

In real terms, Ambedkar was the person who fought against all types of exclusion and promoted the inclusive policies, viz., abolition of untouchability, reservation in education and jobs, property rights for women, etc. These policies forwarded through the Constitution of India promoted the development of SCs, STs and OBCs, in particular. Besides these inclusive policies, Ambedkar also tried to introduce the inclusive policies regarding agricultural sector and industrial sector. In order to benefit the poor farmer and general public, Ambedkar had a blueprint for the developmental model. This chapter discusses the model of Ambedkar with respect to only agriculture.

## Ambedkar's Thoughts on Inclusive Policies in Agriculture

Ambedkar had argued and fought against social exclusion and had promoted inclusion process all along. Even before independence, he had led agitations, which were conducted for the purpose of inclusion of weaker sections in the mainstream. The Chowdar Tank Protest (1927), the Poona Pact (1932) and the Conversion (1956), were some of the important activities which were aimed at inclusion of the untouchables. Besides these, Ambedkar demanded number of constitutional and political safeguards for the weaker sections, which can be appreciated as inclusive policies.

Reservation is one of the inclusion policies, which benefited the weaker section. Ambedkar's thoughts on inclusion policies can be discussed in more than one way.

Ambedkar was an economist. He had emphasized that the role of state is important regarding the inclusion of weaker section. He argued that the state has to play a crucial role in restructuring the society under democratic polity, and the foundation of democracy would be feeble and shaky if there was no social and economic democracy consistent with political democracy (*Babasaheb Ambedkar: Writings and Speeches,* Vol. I, p. 409). In order to promote inclusive growth, he proposed an innovative model of development, which could be a solution to the Indian society, where social and economic inequality was based on the caste structure. Ambedkar gave his thoughts on agriculture and industry, which could be used for the development of society. In this context, Ambedkar's thoughts on the agriculture sector, which promoted inclusion policies, are worth discussing.

Ambedkar's thoughts on Indian agriculture promoted the inclusive policies in India and benefited lakhs of tenants and the farmers directly and indirectly. One important inclusive policy brought out by Ambedkar was abolition of Khoti system, long back in 1937. There was a system of Khoti in Ratnagiri, Colaba (now Raigad) and Thane districts. The khots were appointed to collect the revenue from the tenants and to pay to the government. In social and economic terms, the khots were superior and the tenants were inferior. The khoti system was similar to zamindari system. Since the khots had the power to collect the revenue, they exploited the tenants. In order to have a share in the revenue, the khots were forcing the tenants to pay a higher rate of revenue. This was an exploitation which continued for years. The tenants were suffering under heavy burden.

Since they were poor, it was hard for them to pay the revenue. Many of them were living in abject poverty. Thus, the relation between the Khots and the tenants was bitter and it resulted in social tension. Three Khots were murdered in course of time.

In a way, the tenants were excluded from the mainstream due to a system prevalent from earlier times. Ambedkar played an important role to promote the inclusive policy for tenants through the abolition of khoti system. He introduced a bill for the abolition of the khoti system in the Bombay Legislative Council in 1937 and the bill was passed. Thus, the exploitation of tenants came to an end (*Babasaheb Ambedkar: Writings and Speeches*, Vol. II, pp. 96–103). The exclusion process for the tenants was discontinued and Ambedkar was instrumental in bringing the tenants in the orbit of development by promoting the inclusive policy. This was the first structural inclusive policy for the tenants introduced by Ambedkar. This inclusive policy, which benefited the thousands of the tenants, served as base for the land reforms, that were introduced after independence. The land reforms, which started after 1948, introduced the abolition of intermediatery system prevalent in all the states of India. By this reform, 30 lakh tenants became free from the system. Ambedkar's thoughts on inclusion of tenants in the mainstream was forwarded after the independence. In other words, Ambedkar discontinued a process of exclusion and promoted the inclusive policy, which benefited all the tenants in India.

Ambedkar had prepared a model of economic development, which took into account the majority of the people of this country. The country was facing a problem of economic inequality. Large number of people were excluded from all types of economic assets, especially agricultural land. The SCs and STs were socially and economically excluded. The OBCs also were in the same situation. Ambedkar wanted to discontinue the process of exclusion by promoting the inclusive policies. For this, he prepared a memorandum called 'States and Minorities'. This memorandum was prepared on behalf of the All India Scheduled Castes Federation and was submitted to the Constituent Assembly in 1946. This memorandum was a set of inclusive policies. They were:

- The agriculture sector must be owned by the state.
- The state shall divide the land acquired into farms of standard size and let out the farm for cultivation to residents of village as tenants.
- The farms shall be cultivated as collective farms.
- The farm shall be cultivated as per the rules and directions issued by the government.
- The tenants shall share among themselves, in the manner prescribed, the produce of the farm left after the payment of charges properly leviable on the farm.
- The farm shall be divided among the villagers without distinction of caste or creed and in such manner that there would be no landlord, no tenant and no landless labourers.
- The state shall finance the cultivation of collective farms through the supply of water, implements, manure, seed, etc.
- The state will be entitled to levy in case of the following charges:
    - a portion for land revenue,
    - a portion to pay debenture holders, and
    - a portion to pay for the use of supplied capital goods.

- The state shall prescribe the penalties against the tenants for violation of rules and directions of the government.

Ambedkar developed the above model in order to promote the inclusive growth in India. The intensity of social and economic exclusion was higher in India. Therefore, there was urgency to introduce the inclusive policies, which could benefit large number of people. Furthermore, he wanted to implement these inclusive policies as soon as possible or within ten years. Ambedkar called this model as state socialism. He tried to create equality in the society. He tried to discourage discrimination on any ground. He tried to discontinue the process of exclusion created on the basis of caste system. He tried to promote the inclusion process for the weaker section. Ambedkar further argued that if democracy was to live up to its principle of one man one value, then it was essential to define both the economic structure as well as the political structure of society by the law of constitution (*Babasaheb Ambedkar: Writings and Speeches,* Vol. I, pp. 396–397).

But, the Constituent Assembly could not support the memorandum or the set of inclusive policies regarding agriculture, and hence Ambedkar could not incorporate this model of development under the Constitution. Thus, the model of inclusive growth came to an end.

## Consequences of Refusal to Ambedkar's Model

The refusal to the inclusive growth model of Ambedkar created a number of economic problems in the post-independence period. As on today, the present situation of Indian agriculture represents the highest state of inequality. Some of the consequences can be listed as below:

1. The inequality that existed before the independence continued even after independence. The caste system and the discrimination system were protected. The economic capital was determined on the basis of caste system, which was unjust and inhuman.
2. The process of exclusion of SCs and STs continued even after the independence.
3. The weaker section remains in poverty even now. The Planning Commission (2007) has also accepted this grim fact. The Commission argued that, 'the major weakness in the economy is that growth is not perceived as being sufficiently inclusive for many groups, especially Scheduled Castes, Scheduled Tribes and minorities'.
4. The concept of inclusive growth is now being discussed at all levels. The Planning Commission (2007) and the state agency has been highlighting the inclusive growth. Ambedkar had thought about such an idea of growth even before the independence.
5. The agricultural policies after the independence promoted the exclusion process. The economic situation and various schemes have been struggling to create the inclusive growth. But, this has been impossible. The agricultural policies benefited the landlord.
6. The refusal to Ambedkar's model of inclusive growth of the agricultural sector has protected the inequality persisting in the agricultural sector regarding the size of operational holding. For example, 'in the year 1970–71, out of all land holdings in the country, 85 per cent of the land holdings were falling under the category of small and marginal holdings, which was sharing just 40 per

cent of the total agricultural land. As against this, 15 per cent of the land holding was falling under the category of medium and large holdings, which was sharing 60 per cent of the total agricultural area'.

7. There has been high economic deprivation among the SCs and STs. The deprivation has been created by the system. In other words, the process of economic exclusion of weaker sections has been sponsored by the state.

8. Ambedkar wanted to create a non-discriminative economic system. Agriculture has been the backbone of Indian economy. The dependency on agriculture has been high. This was the single source of survival in the rural area. Due to refusal to Ambedkar's model, the excluded groups could not get any source of survival, which created a number of unrests in the country.

9. The problem of the Naxalites is also one of the consequences of the refusal to the socio-economic equality, which Ambedkar had expected. The Naxalite problem has been increasing in recent years. 'The Naxals problem has strong socio-economic roots in the failure of social administration to satisfy the basic needs of the local population. The Naxal organizations have expanded their influence in 55 districts of 9 states in 2003, which further increased to 155 districts of 15 states in 2005. The tribals are part of this group' (Paul, 2006). The tribals are away from the fruits of the development. They want their share in the development. However, their ways and methods of demanding justice and development cannot be justified at any cost. The main base of this problem is unequal distribution of wealth. The state socialism or the nationalization of agriculture could have given proper representation to

the tribals. They could have been a part of the development. (The reservation policy has brought some of the tribals in the mainstream).

10. The social inequality which in turn created the economic inequality remains the obstacle for the development. India has been struggling to establish itself as a developed country. But, because of existing inequality in agriculture and in all the other sectors India could not develop.
11. The social and economic injustice to the SCs could be perceived before the independence and even after it. The dependency of SCs on the upper caste farmers continued which resulted into exploitation and atrocities.

Thus, due to the refusal to Ambedkar's model of development in agriculture, there have been direct and indirect, seen and unseen, undesirable consequences. These could have been avoided.

## Conclusion

Ambedkar's thoughts on agriculture are expressed as the set of inclusion policies, which were formulated to benefit a large number of tenants and farmers. Furthermore, if his thoughts as state owned agriculture were accepted, it could have brought revolutionary changes in the Indian society. The society could have come to terms with economic equality. There would not have been economic problems in Indian agriculture and the society. Since Ambedkar had a grand vision, he had planned a viable model of the development, where there was place for all the sections of the society. But, this model was not accepted and it resulted in a number of economic and social problems. Agriculture has been the most important sector for India, but riddled with unequal distribution of land and regional disparities. Thus, there is an urgent need to rethink Ambedkar's thoughts on agriculture.

## References

*Ambedkar Babasaheb: Writings and Speeches,* Vol. I, Department of Education, Government of Maharashtra Publication, Mumbai.

*Ambedkar Babasaheb: Writings and Speeches,* Vol. II, Government of Maharashtra Publication, Mumbai.

Planning Commission (2007), Eleventh Five-Year Plan (2007–12), Vol. I, Government of India Publication, New Delhi.

Paul, P. (2006), Security Research Review (www.bharat-rakshak.com).

Todman, Lynn (2004), *Reflections on Social Exclusion* (Italy).

## Chapter 4

# Ambedkar and Exclusion and Inclusion of the Scheduled Castes

### An Analysis of the Reservation Status in Central Government

Social inclusion is a strategy to fight against the demerits of exclusion existing in the society. The process of inclusion can promote equality and discourage inequality. The social inclusion strategy can be framed as per the type and degree of exclusion. The social exclusion in India is based on the caste system which has created the highest degree of social and economic inequality. This inequality has continued for years. After the independence, Ambedkar fought against social exclusion and sought out to promote the process of inclusion. The Government of India introduced a number of inclusive policies for the development of backward castes.

We now propose to deal with the reservation policy for Scheduled Castes (SCs), especially in the central government sector, and explain the social exclusion of the SCs, and also the inclusive policy, i.e., reservation policy and the obstacles in the process of implementation. In the end, we hope to throw some light on the contemporary effects of exclusion and inclusion with respect to the SCs.

## Social and Economic Deprivation of Scheduled Castes

The social and economic exclusion in Indian society is most common. The roots of such exclusion could be traced to the social history. The caste system has unique features among the systems of social stratification. Every Hindu necessarily belongs to the caste of his parents and in that caste he inevitably remains. No accumulation of wealth and no exercise of talents can alter one's caste position. The caste system has no basis in Hindu religion and is a product of Hindu traditional law and of the weakness of the central political authority during much of India's history (Panikkar, 1955: 121). The caste system of India is very complex even in contemporary period; it can be understood through reviewing the ancient period of Indian caste system. The Indian society was divided into four varnas, viz., Brahmin, Kshatriya, Vaishya and Sudra. The first three varnas were twice born, while the Sudra was born only once (Kamble, 1982: 8–9). The *Manusmriti* imposed several social restrictions on the Sudras and placed them in the lowest position in ritual purity (ibid., 20). The Sudras have suffered social and economic inequity since ages and hence the concept of pollution was attached to them, they were treated as untouchable people. The Sudras were known with variety of nomenclature in the ancient and modern India. Some of them are: untouchables, Sudras, Atisudras, Panchamas, Harijans, Dalits, Depressed Castes, etc.

The untouchable castes were systematically listed in the 1931 Census of India and were officially defined as Depressed Castes in 1932 (Harold, 1965: 35). These enlisted castes were named as Scheduled Castes for the first time by the Simon Commission and it was mentioned in the Government of India Act 1935. The Government of India published a list of Scheduled Castes under the Government of India (Scheduled Castes) Order 1936 (Kamble, 1982: 31).

After the adoption of the Constitution, the Government of India issued the Constitution (Scheduled Castes) Order, 1950.

The social restrictions imposed on SCs in ancient period continued even in the post-independence period with declining intensity. Social discrimination and economic disabilities have strong relation in Indian caste system (Myrdal, 1968). This led to higher level of social and economic deprivation in the case of SCs. This deprivation could be found even among the Scheduled Tribes (STs), denotified tribes and Other Backward Castes (OBCs). The social and economic deprivation of SCs has been higher; since they were socially excluded from the normal society. The process of exclusion continued for hundreds of years, which created social barriers within the society. As a result, the deprivation continued even after independence.

SCs account for 179.7 million people that represented 17.5 per cent of the total population of India in 2001 (Five-Year Plan: 2001–02: 405). The decadal growth of SCs (India) in 1991 was 30 per cent, which was more than the decadal general population growth (ibid., 419). Eighty-one per cent of SCs are living in rural area (ibid.). Uttar Pradesh alone accounts for 21.2 per cent of the total SC population. Nearly 84 per cent of SC population live in ten states, viz., Andhra Pradesh (7.7%), Bihar (9.1%), Karnataka (5.3%), Kerala (2.1%), Madhya Pradesh (7%), Maharashtra (6.3%), Rajasthan (5.5%), Tamil Nadu (7.8%), Uttar Pradesh (21.2%) and West Bengal (11.6%) (ibid., 405). In a few states, they constitute more than 20 per cent of the state's total population, viz., Punjab (28.3%), Himachal Pradesh (25.3%), West Bengal (23.6%), Uttar Pradesh (21%) (ibid., 405–406). Despite having significant strength in the total population, the SCs are victims of caste system. They have been socially and economically excluded from all types of opportunities. In order to promote the development of SCs, the Government of India introduced reservation policy in the government sector. This is stated as one of the important inclusive policy.

## Reservation Policy: An Inclusive Policy

The social and economic deprivation among SCs had been most common during pre- and post-independence periods due to the social exclusion imposed by the Hindu social system. Therefore, there was a need of inclusive policies for the development of SCs. The Constitution of India promoted the inclusive policies in the post-independence period. One of that is reservation policy in the government recruitment. The objective of this inclusive policy is to eradicate the social and economic disparities in the society.

Article 15 (4) and 16 (4) of the Indian Constitution has made provisions of reservation for backward classes in educational institutions and public employment. The reservation policy has to be followed by both central and state governments. The person behind this was Ambedkar, the framer of the Indian Constitution. The reservation policy was accepted by the government. The social and economic upliftment of SCs could be made through the reservation policy. Social exclusion is a product of Hindu caste system. Hence, inclusive policy like reservation policy has been promoted. The Government of India has been following this policy in recruitment and also in education. The reservation policy has been a base for the development of SCs in India. The inclusive policy like reservation policy in the government sector has promoted the development of SCs to some extent.

However, there has been scanty implementation of reservation policy as defined by the Constitution of India.

The central government recruitment has been an important and the largest area, where the reservation policy could be implemented effectively. But, over the years, the position of reservation in this area has been weak. Generally, the posts can be classified into four classes, namely, Class I, Class II, Class III and Class IV. The Class I posts are very important, which are involved in the decision-making process. Whereas, Class II posts are also equally important. But, Class III and Class IV posts are classified as inferior posts. It includes peons, sweepers, etc.

Over the years, the representation of SCs in Class I posts has been increasing at a steady rate. It was just 0.35 per cent of the total number of posts in 1953, which reached to 1.64 per cent in 1965. Due to the social exclusion imposed on SCs by the Hindu caste system, initially, after the independence, the educational position of SCs was very poor. But, as the Constitution of India supported the various inclusive policies, which can be called as the safeguards to the SCs, the educational level gradually increased. However, the implementation of reservation in the Class I posts remained low. In the years 1970 and 1975, the reservation level was 2.36 per cent and 3.43 per cent respectively. In the later period, i.e., in the year 1992, it was 9.70 per cent and finally it reached to 10.13 per cent in 1995. The prescribed quota of reservation for SCs is 15 per cent of the total posts. Yet, there remains a backlog of about 4.87 per cent of the total. At national level, this figure includes thousands of posts. It means that the SCs are still socially excluded from the decision-making process. Similar trend can be found in Class II posts, where the representation of SCs was 1.29 per cent in 1953, which reached to 2.82 per cent in 1965, 3.84 per cent in 1970, 11.60 per cent in 1992 and finally to 13.13 per cent in 1995. In the classified form of posts, the backlog is 1.87

per cent of the total posts. Altogether, Class I and Class II posts' backlog in the reservation has been highly unsatisfactory (Social Welfare Committee for SCs/STs Report: 1999–2000).

**Table 1**

*Reservation Status of Scheduled Castes in Central Government Recruitment*

| *Year* | *Class I* | *Class II* | *Class III* | *Class IV* |
|---|---|---|---|---|
| 1953 | 0.35 | 1.29 | 4.52 | 20.52 |
| 1965 | 1.64 | 2.82 | 8.88 | 17.73 |
| 1970 | 2.36 | 3.84 | 9.27 | 18.09 |
| 1975 | 3.43 | 4.98 | 10.27 | 18.64 |
| 1979 | 4.83 | 8.07 | 11.54 | 19.16 |
| 1992 | 9.70 | 11.60 | 15.80 | 20.70 |
| 1995 | 10.13 | 13.13 | 15.46 | 20.46 |
| 2001 | 11.42 | 12.82 | 16.12 | 17.89 |
| 2003 | 11.93 | 14.32 | 16.29 | 17.89 |

*Sources:* 1. Department of Personnel, Government of India Report: 1993.
2. Social Welfare Committee for SCs/STs Report: 1999–2000/2005–06.

The reservation status of SCs in Class III posts in 1953 was 4.52 per cent, which increased to 15.46 per cent in 1995. The representation in the present era is satisfactory. More interestingly, in Class IV, the representation of SCs has been higher from the beginning, i.e., in the year 1953, it was 20.52 per cent and in the year 1995, it was 20.46 per cent. The reservation status in Class IV has always been more than the requirement. This does not show the efficiency of implementing authority, since only the SC members (also STs) and no one from upper castes apply for such posts. The caste system has percolated in the present structure of employment in the central government. The main part of the reservation policy is that the Class I and II posts' backlog must be filled, which is estimated as around 5 lakh jobs. It shows that in the post-independence period, there has been problems in the implementation of inclusive policy for the development of SCs.

More interestingly, in the recent years, i.e., in 2001, the representation in the Class I, Class II and Class III increased to 11.42 per cent, 12.82 per cent and 16.12 per cent respectively. But, in case of Class IV, the representation fell down to 17.89 per cent as compared to 1995. In 2003, the representation of SCs remained similar as in 2001. This shows that, after 2001, the process of inclusion has been discouraged.

The Hindu caste system imposed a serious social exclusion on SCs for years, but, after the independence, the inclusive policy like reservation policy brought the them in the mainstream at least to some extent. But as per the Constitution of India, the defined inclusive policies must be protected by the state. But, in the recent years, the state has been neglecting such policies in the name of globalization. The system created a number of hurdles in the implementation of reservation policies which could have brought positive changes among the SCs.

## Obstacles in the Inclusive Policies

The Constitution of India states in the Directive Principles that, 'The state shall promote with special care the educational and economic interest of the scheduled castes/tribes and shall protect them from social injustice and all forms of exploitation'. In accordance with these constitutional provisions, number of inclusive policies have been initiated by the government. In the economic, educational and political spheres, inclusive provisions have been made through reservation and representation to improve their access and participation. This is the result of the inclusive policy promoted by the Constitution. The provision of political reservation in various bodies and reservation in government services have promoted the SCs.

However, in the recent years, Indian economy is changing at a dynamic rate. The global economic effects can be seen in the Indian economy. Again, there are a number of evidences which show positive economic growth with negative employment growth. After the onset of globalization, for the last number of years, the growth of employment has been negative which is stated as jobless growth. The Economic Survey 2004–05 has pointed out that, 4.08 crore job seekers were registered with the employment exchanges across the country in 2004. Out of them, only one lakh placements were affected by the employment exchanges at the all-India level in the same year. This trend has been recorded for a number of years, especially after the introduction of the new economic reforms.

Even today vacancies in government posts are not being filled and posts are being abolished. It is estimated that ever since the neo-liberal policies have been implemented there has been a loss of around 10 lakh jobs in the central government which includes abolition of around 7 lakh posts and unfilled vacancies in around 3 to 4 lakh posts. There are an additional 15 lakh posts in the state government services which have remained vacant. Apart from aggravating the unemployment situation, this policy has had a direct impact on SC employment also as it shows a decline in the jobs reserved for these sections.

A large number of posts have been wiped out by the government itself. This has adversely affected the SCs. There has been a big backlog. Instead of filling the posts, if the posts are abolished, then it will create a limitation in the development of SCs. Reservation in the government recruitment has been the base for the development of SCs. This has been the best inclusive policy for the development. But, globalization has created a threat for such an inclusive policy. Therefore, this disparity has affected adversely the social, economic and cultural life of the SCs. According to the report of the Working Group on the Empowering of SCs, over 1,13,450 job opportunities were lost by the Scheduled Castes in the central government during the period 1992–97 (Tenth Five-Year Plan: 2002–07). Eradication of reservation posts on a large scale could be seen in all the state governments. So far it is estimated that around 5 lakh posts in various state governments have been abolished. The reasons for taking such steps are told as excess recruitment, globalization, efficiency, etc. During the last few years, several lakhs of reserved posts have been wiped out. Majority of these posts were high class posts, which could have played an important role in the determination of the economic position of the society. The Constitution of India guarantees the protection of SCs on the ground of educational and economic interests and also protects them from social injustice. Reservation policy is defined in the Constitution. Without filling the posts of SCs, if the posts are abolished, then it is a clear violation of the Constitution.

The inclusive policy, like reservation, which has been the base for the development of SCs, is also being neglected by the states in the name of globalization. If the state is neglecting this inclusive policy, it shows that the state is pushing again the SCs to the process of social exclusion. The SCs are socially and economically deprived, hence there must be strict implementation of the inclusive policy.

## Conclusion

Over the years, all the branches of the government sectors have been neglecting the reservation policy. Even after sixty-five years of independence, the reservation status of

SCs in all of the government branches has been unsatisfactory. The reservation policy which is stated as the most important inclusive policy has been underutilized. The rate of disparity in the implementation has been high. In the phase of globalization, the government is discouraging the reservation policy. This situation has created various social and economic problems in the contemporary period. In a way, the social justice for the SCs has been denied even in the contemporary period. Despite the constitutional provisions, the reservation policy has been neglected. This must be taken as a violation of the Constitution. Neglecting such an inclusive policy would affect adversely the social and economic position of the SCs.

## References

Five-Year Plan (2002–2007), Vol. II, Planning Commission, Government of India.

Harold, Issac (1965), *India's Ex-untouchables,* Asia Publishing House, Bombay.

Kamble, N.D. (1982), *The Scheduled Castes*, Ashish Publishing House, New Delhi.

Kamble, J.R. (1979), *Rise and Awakening of Depressed Classes in India*, National Publishing House, New Delhi.

Khan, Mumtaz Ali (1980), *Scheduled Castes and Their Position in India*, Uppal Publishing House, New Delhi.

Myrdal, Gunnar (1968), *Asian Drama*, Vol. II.

Panikkar, K.M. (1955), *Hindu Society at the Crossroads* Asia Publishing House, Bombay.

Social Welfare Committee for SCs/STs Publisher Report 1999–2000, Government of India.

Tenth Five-Year Plan (2002–07), Government of India Publication.

# Chapter 5

# Ambedkar's Thoughts on Industries and Their Relevance

Ambedkar had offered valuable thoughts and insights related to the industries. He believed that the structure of industries must be organized so that it would benefit all the segments of the society. For this, Ambedkar suggested state socialism. For Ambedkar, state socialism meant the nationalization of agriculture and industry in the restricted areas. Ambedkar stated that agricultural land must be nationalized but, in case of industries he said that only key industries and insurance should be nationalized. Ambedkar was supporting state intervention in the economic system, which can bring about the equitable distribution of resources in the society. He wanted a permanent economic structure of state socialism. He held that the parliamentary democracy alone cannot bring out permanent state socialism. It cannot be achieved even through dictatorship. In this regard, Ambedkar said: 'The way out seems to retain parliamentary democracy and to prescribe state socialism by the law of constitution, so that it will be beyond the reach of a parliamentary majority to suspend amends or abrogate it. It is only by this that one can achieve the triple objects, namely, to establish socialism, retain parliamentary democracy and avoid dictatorship' (*Babasaheb Ambedkar: Writings and Speeches,* Vol. I).

Ambedkar wanted to restructure the Indian agriculture and industry. We propose to discuss the thoughts of Ambedkar on industries and their relevance in the contemporary situation. In the case of industries, he presented the following important thoughts:

- The key industries shall only be owned and run by the state.
- The industries which are not key industries, but which are basic, shall be owned by the state and shall be run by the state or corporation established by the state.
- The insurance sector must be nationalised.

Ambedkar wanted to nationalize only key industries and not all the industries. He also wanted to keep sufficient space for private companies. Thus, he worked towards the establishment of mixed economy. His main intention behind this model was to promote equitable distribution of wealth. The state-owned industries can play an important role in this regard. The private ownership may lead to an unequal distribution of wealth. The state industries can think for the welfare of the people, especially the depressed people. The private industries cannot perform this. There was also another indirect aspect of Ambedkar's thoughts regarding industries. The process of industrialization may absorb the disguised unemployment from the agriculture sector. Therefore, Ambedkar insisted to establish the key industries under the state control.

Ambedkar held that insurance was equally important for the welfare of the people. He suggested that the insurance sector should be owned and run by the state only. Life insurance owned by the state may provide security to the people.

Ambedkar also laid down some clauses in the Directive Principles which support the equal distribution of wealth and means of production. These can be stated as below:

'The state shall, in particular, direct its policy toward securing:

(a) that citizens, men and women equally have the right to an adequate means of livelihood;

(b) that the ownership and control of the resources of the community are so distributed as best to subserve the common good;

(c) that the operation of the economic system does not result in the concentration of wealth and means of production to the common detriment.'

As per Ambedkar's thoughts and the Directive Principles of the Constitution of India, the Planning Commission of India set a few long-term objectives, one of which is to set up a socialistic society based on equality and justice and the absence of exploitation.

## Implementation of Ambedkar's Thoughts

Ambedkar's thoughts on industries and insurance could be traced to the industrial policies declared in the post-independence period. His thoughts can be seen in the process of the structuring of economy and the industrial policies. Unfortunately, many experts have neglected Ambedkar's contribution in building the structure of the economy. There are a number of evidences to show that he has influenced the economic system and industrial policies in the post-independence period.

As per the Directive Principles of the Constitution of India and Ambedkar's thoughts, in the Industrial Policy Resolution of 1956, three categories were introduced. In the first category were included such industries which would be the exclusive responsibility of the state. In the second category were included such industries which would be progressively state owned, but the private sector may be permitted to supplement the efforts of the state. This is well known as mixed economy. The state-owned industries can prevent the rise of monopoly ownership and exploitation which are inherent in the private sector. However, the private industries were also given important place and were expected to function in harmony with the overall aims and policies of economic planning.

The Industrial Policy Resolution, 1956 had the following important provisions for the classification of industries into three categories:

(a) *Schedule A:* those which were to be an exclusive responsibility of the state.
(b) *Schedule B:* those which were to be progressively state owned and in which the state would generally set up new enterprises, but in which private enterprise would be expected only to supplement the effort of the state, and
(c) *Schedule C:* all the remaining industries and their future development would, in general, be left to the initiative and enterprise of the private sector.

The importance of the state-owned industries was understood by Ambedkar, therefore he was insisting on it. In the post-independence period, the state-owned industries have tried their best to perform according to the Directive Principles of the Constitution of India. Of course, there have been some limitations in the functioning of these industries. And, these limitations are found in the implementation authority.

The objectives of the public sector or state-owned industries are as follows:

(a) to promote rapid economic development through creation and expansion of infrastructure.
(b) to generate financial resources for development.
(c) to promote redistribution of income and wealth.
(d) to create employment opportunities.
(e) to promote balanced regional growth.
(f) to encourage the development of small-scale and ancillary industries, and
(g) to promote exports on the one side and import substitution on the other.

Some of the contributions of the state-owned industries can be described as:

- The state industries have been an important source of employment in the total employment. It was estimated as 111 lakhs in the year 1971 which increased to 155 lakhs in 1981 and 191 lakhs in 1991. But after 1991, the employment level in the public sector has been decreasing. In the year 2004, the total employment was 182 lakhs (Economic Survey: 2006–07).
- The state-owned industries have played an important role in the net domestic product. About 7.5 per cent of the net domestic product was coming from the state-owned industries (altogether) in the year 1951, which further increased to 23 per cent in the year 1991–92 (Tenth Five-Year Plan Proceedings).
- The state-owned industries have played a significant role in developing the key sectors and the infrastructure of the economy, e.g., railways, roads, irrigation, power, iron and steel, oil, etc.
- The state-owned industries have promoted industrialization in India. It has entered into a wide range of

industries and products from basic goods to capital goods like steel, coal, copper, zinc, minerals, heavy machinery, drugs, fertilizers, chemical, etc. These industries have in turn promoted the private industries too.

- The state-owned industries have been an important source of employment for the weaker sections. The representation of the Scheduled Castesn (SCs) and Scheduled Tribes (STs) can be seen in these industries. It is a fact that the representation of the SCs/STs is not given as per the Constitution of India. But, Ambedkar's thoughts about promoting the social and economic equality through the state-owned industries can be observed in the post-independence period.
- The state-owned industries have played an important role in promoting the social and economic welfare. They tried to redistribute the income and wealth of the society. However, there has been a number of obstacles in the implementation which resulted into serious drawbacks. But, at normal range, as a whole, it can be said that Ambedkar's state socialism in the industry has resulted in benefiting a large section of the people.

## Conclusion

The state-owned industries have benefited the society both directly and indirectly. Ambedkar's thoughts have been efficacious for the Indian society. Furthermore, the insurance sector was also nationalized. Life insurance is provided by the state. This has benefited large sections of the people, giving security to majority of the people. Up to 1991, Ambedkar's thoughts had strong relevance with respect to the economic structure and policies in India. But after 1991, globalization has changed the basic structure of the economy which has resulted in/caused serious consequences. The state intervention has been reduced to a great extent. This has resulted in the serious exploitation of the society. Importance is now being given to the private sector. Some of the state-owned industries have also been sold to the private sector. The private sector has been allowed in the insurance sector too. Thus, the role of the state-owned industries has been reduced. In the present economic system, the private enterprises are given more importance. One of the important changes is that the state has reduced the number of key industries from seventeen to eight. Most of the state-owned industries have been privatized, either partially or completely. Foreign investment is allowed in many industries with least intervention of the government. The reason for deinvesting the state-owned industries is their sickness. As a whole, this has resulted into high rate of unemployment, exploitation, insecurity, inflation, trade cycles, etc. This has created a social instability. Therefore, once again, there is a need to rethink about the state intervention in the most essential sectors which promote social and economic equality. The demerits of globalization can be removed by accepting the thoughts of Ambedkar.

## References

*Babasaheb Ambedkar: Writings and Speech*, Vol. I, Government of Maharashtra Publication, Mumbai.

Economic Survey (2006–07), Government of India Publication, New Delhi.

Tenth Five-Year Plan proceedings (2002–2007), Government of India Publication, New Delhi.

## Chapter 6

# Ambedkar's Thoughts and the Development of the Buddhists

Ambedkar embraced Buddhism on 14th October 1956 at Nagpur. Along with him lakhs of his followers also embraced Buddhism. The decision of conversion to Buddhism was revolutionary. Ambedkar had given hints of conversion long back in 1935. After the detailed study of various religions, he finally decided to embrace Buddhism. Unfortunately, after the conversion ceremony (1956), Ambedkar died. This was a great shock for the Ambedkarites. In the post-Ambedkar period, many Ambedkarites have tried to spread Buddhism. Some of them have arranged conversion (to Buddhism) ceremonies. Recently Uditraj, an eminent activist also tried to organize such ceremonies. Of course, a number of criticisms were made. Buddhism as a religion could not spread in India, however, in Maharashtra, it got an important place. The Mahars of Maharashtra accepted Ambedkar's philosophy along with Buddhism. In the contemporary period, the Mahars were known as neo-Buddhists (though the author prefers to call them as Buddhists instead of neo-Buddhists). The religious conversion (to Buddhism) has brought a number of social, cultural and economic effects among the Buddhists in

Maharashtra. Ambedkar's Buddhism has changed the social and economic philosophy of the Buddhists. It has taught them rational thinking. As per the message of Ambedkar, the Buddhists have accepted the process of migration to the urban areas. The famous message of Ambedkar, 'Educate, Agitate and Organize' has brought revolutionary changes among the Buddhists. Comparatively, the Buddhists have achieved good social, cultural and economic status. It is a fact that a large majority of the Buddhists are living in poverty. Their social and economic condition is not satisfactory. However, there exists a small group of people among the Buddhists who have achieved good status. This group can be seen in the urban area, especially in Mumbai. This group of people constitute higher middle class. The number of such people is small as compared to the whole Buddhist society, however they are important since they have created a perfect development model based on Ambedkarism. This model of development can inspire other people within the Buddhists and also other than the Buddhists. All the backward communities can benefit from this model of development.

The main content of the model of development is migration, education and conversion. The Buddhists who have created this model are living with self-dignity, social confidence and special social identity. As a whole, the model is nothing but the process of overall development of the Buddhists. We want to explain the relationship between the thoughts of Ambedkar and the development of the Buddhists in Maharashtra. We have selected the city of Mumbai as the area of study. Mumbai is a place where great many employment opportunities are available and where migration can be seen. Thus, Mumbai has been an important place for Ambedkarites' movement. We have collected the information from 166 samples (Buddhist males and females). The information of these samples has been processed and compiled through various matrimony websites, specially dedicated to the arrangements of the marriages. All the samples were registered with one or the other of these websites. Out of 200 registered samples, about 166 samples are related (101 males and 65 females) on the basis of purposive sampling method. The condition of selecting samples was that the sample must be born in Maharashtra. The analysis based on these samples is representative. This cannot be applied to all the Buddhists living in Maharashtra.

## Analysis

Ambedkar had always tried to organize all the untouchables like Mahars, Matangs, Chamars and the others. However, only the Mahars were serious about his thoughts. The Mahars were the real followers of Ambedkar's thoughts. Though, there were also followers among the Matangs and the Chamars. But, in comparison with the Mahars, the number was less. Ambedkar's thoughts on migration, education and conversion were accepted by the Mahars, whereas the Matangs and the Chamars rejected them. The Mahars gave up their traditional occupations and migrated to urban areas. They got employment. Their next generation went for higher education. As a result, the Mahars established themselves as the Buddhists with satisfactory educational status. G.G. Wankhede (2001) also has pointed out that the Mahars have achieved better educational status than the Matangs and the Chamars. The main reason for this is that these latter communities remained away from Ambedkarite movements. The Matangs and the Chamars continued to practise their traditional occupations. In contrast, the Mahars or today's Buddhists have gone for revolutionary changes. They have created their separate social and cultural identity. Many scholars across the world have been attracted towards these changes. They have studied the socio-cultural changes among the Buddhists.

Kantowsky (2001) has described the Buddhists of Maharashtra as below:

> ... on the level of commerce, neo-Buddhists, most of whom came from the traditionally untouchable, the Mahar caste, try to refuse the discriminating impure position...
>
> ... on the level of commensality, the neo-Buddhists have changed their eating, drinking habits publicly according to the percepts...

On the basis of the available studies, the following conclusions can be drawn:

- Large majority of the people, who have embraced Buddhism are from the Mahar community.
- The Buddhists (the ex-untouchables) have refused to endorse the tradition of Hindu caste system.
- The Buddhists have established a new identity, which is contrary to Hindu society.

The socio-cultural and economic changes among the Buddhists is a result of Ambedkar's thoughts. The credit should also be given to the Ambedkarites movement carried out in Maharashtra by all the Republican parties. The base of the movement has been Ambedkarism for a number of years (Recently, there have been a number of socio-political adjustments in the movement. Since this topic is different, it has not been discussed here. However, a brief discussion is given in the eighth chapter of this book). The present context seeks to study the positive relationship between Ambedkar's thoughts and the development of the Buddhists. As today, large majority of the Buddhists are living in poverty. In the urban area or the cities, majority of them are living in slums. However, there is a group of people with lower strength in Mumbai, which can be described as the higher middle class. They have achieved good educational status, which helps them to get good jobs. The occupational and income status of this group has been remarkable. They have created an ideal model, which can guide and inspire the other backward communities.

The occupational status is also interesting among the selected Buddhists of Mumbai. All the Mahars follow the Buddhist culture, which is contrary to the Hindu culture. Some of them have embraced Buddhism and some of them have not, yet they follow it. There is an insignificant size of population, which have been practising Hindu culture. However, Ambedkar has given a revolutionary turn to Buddhism, which is followed by every Ambedkarite. It is believed that the real Ambedkarites are those who follow Ambedkarism along with Buddhism. This can be seen in India, especially in Maharashtra. Ambedkar's Buddhism has brought revolutionary changes among the Mahars. The Mahars have changed their identity with the help of conversion. Even prior to conversion, Ambedkar had given the very important thought, i.e., 'Educate, Agitate and Organize'. As a result, the Mahars of Maharashtra have accepted the thoughts of Ambedkar, which have brought development among them. Hence, the Mahars have become Buddhists. We seek to explain the positive impact of Ambedkar's thoughts. All the educational and economic development are linked with Buddhism or conversion. Therefore, effects may be described as the result of the conversion.

Out of the selected 166 samples (Buddhists), 100 per cent of them have identified themselves as Buddhists. Among them, the understanding of Buddhism seems to be clear. Almost 98 per cent of the samples have received at least graduation degrees. Out of which, 12 per cent and 10 per cent of the selected Buddhists have obtained BA and MA degrees respectively. About 24 per cent of them have obtained computer and information technology related degrees. Another 26 per cent of them have obtained MBA degrees. Whereas, 8 per cent and 10 per cent of the selected Buddhists have obtained medical and engineering degrees respectively. Most important fact is that there is a significant representation of women in computer related degrees. As a whole, the selected Buddhists have obtained a variety of degrees. Out of the total selected Buddhists, 50 per cent of them have obtained modern degrees. This shows that they are changing with the time. The acquiring of traditional degrees like BA/MA has now declined. The professional degrees are more popular among them. In the phase of globalization, such a positive change is necessary to survive economically.

Among the total selected Buddhists, 10 per cent of them are school and college teachers. Teaching is most common among the Buddhists and other Scheduled Castes (SCs). However, in recent times, there have been changes in the occupations corresponding to the changes in education. In this regard, 17 per cent of the selected Buddhists have computer related jobs and 7.5 per cent of the samples are working in the information technology sector. Most important is that 25 per cent of the selected Buddhists are working as business executives in various companies. Remaining 12 per cent, 8.5 per cent and 4 per cent are working as doctors, engineers and advocates respectively.

Besides these, 2 per cent and 3 per cent of the selected samples are working in interior designing and advertising field respectively. Interestingly, the representation of women is significant. Among the total selected women, 24.5 per cent, 18 per cent and again 18 per cent are working as business executives, doctors and in computer related jobs respectively. This occupational structure indicates that the Buddhists with higher education, who are living in Mumbai, have developed themselves.

The income status among the selected Buddhists is also interesting. On account of their higher education, they have obtained higher level of employment. They are working in different sectors with higher skill. Hence, their income level is also high. Out of the total selected Buddhists, 4.5 per cent of the samples are earning a monthly income of Rs 5,000, whereas 15 per cent of the samples are earning a monthly income between Rs 5,001 to Rs 10,000. Majority of the selected samples (58%) are earning between Rs 10,001 to Rs 20,000. Remaining 25 per cent and 2 per cent are earning between Rs 20,001 to Rs 25,000 and Rs 25,001 to Rs 30,000 respectively. There is a good representation of women in the higher income group. Majority of the selected women (57.5%) are earning a monthly income between Rs 10,000 to Rs 20,000. The highest income earners are business executives. In terms of annual income, 5 per cent of the selected samples are earning an annual income between Rs 60,000 to Rs 1,00,000. Majority of the samples (54%) are earning between Rs 1,50,001 to Rs 2,00,000. The highest level of income is between Rs 2,50,001 to Rs 3,50,000 per year.

The most important and positive side is that all the selected samples (100%), who belong to the Mahar community, have accepted the Buddhist culture. It means that the old social identity of the Ambedkarites has been wiped out and they have created a new social identity. The base of this identity is nothing but Ambedkarism.

**Table 1**

*Occupational Structure among the Selected Buddhists in Mumbai*

(in %)

| *Occupation* | *Males* | *Females* | *Total* |
|---|---|---|---|
| Clerk | 7 | 4.5 | 5.5 |
| Teacher | 5 | 4.5 | 5 |
| Lecturer | 7 | 2 | 5 |
| Computer | 16 | 18 | 17 |
| Information Technology | 8 | 6.5 | 7.5 |
| Business Executives | 26 | 24.5 | 25 |
| Doctor | 8 | 18 | 12 |
| Engineer | 10 | 6.5 | 8.5 |
| Advocate | 3 | 4.5 | 4 |
| Accountant | 2 | — | 2 |
| Interior Designing | 2 | 2 | 2 |
| Advertising | 3 | — | 3 |
| Beauty Parlour | — | 4.5 | 2 |
| Fashion Designing | — | 4.5 | 2 |
| Research | 3 | — | 2 |
| Total | 100 | 100 | 100 |

*Note:* Some figures are rounded up to two decimal.

*Source:* Compiled data on the basis of information available on Bharat Matrimony.

**Table 2**

*Monthly Income of Selected Buddhists in Mumbai*

(in %)

| *Income Level (Rs)* | *Males* | *Females* | *Total* |
|---|---|---|---|
| 5,000 | 5 | 5 | 4.5 |
| 5,001 to 10,000 | 13 | 15.5 | 14 |
| 10,001 to 20,000 | 52 | 57.5 | 54.5 |
| 20,001 to 25,000 | 26 | 22 | 25 |
| 25,001 to 30,000 | 4 | — | 2 |
| Total | 100 | 100 | 100 |

*Note:* Some figures are rounded up to two decimal.

*Source:* Compiled data on the basis of information available on Bharat Matrimony.

**Table 3**

*Annual Income of Selected Buddhists in Mumbai*

(in %)

| *Income Level (Rs)* | *Males* | *Females* | *Total* |
|---|---|---|---|
| 60,000 to 1,00,000 | 5 | 5 | 5.5 |
| 1,00,001 to 1,50,000 | 13 | 15.5 | 14 |
| 1,50,001 to 2,00,000 | 52 | 57.5 | 54 |
| 2,00,001 to 2,50,000 | 26 | 22 | 25 |
| 2,50,001 to 3,50,000 | 4 | — | 2 |
| Total | 100 | 100 | 100 |

*Note:* Some figures are rounded up to two decimal.

*Source:* Compiled data on the basis of information available on Bharat Matrimony.

## Conclusion

(a) The available studies have shown that there has been migration of the Buddhists from the rural to urban areas and the rate of migration has been high.

(b) The Buddhists living in the urban areas, especially in Mumbai, have established their separate social, cultural and economic identity. The identity of Buddhists is contrary to the Hindu castes.

(c) It is a fact that the majority of the Buddhists, especially the rural Buddhists, are living in poverty. However, there is a small group of Buddhists living in Mumbai, who are from the higher middle class.

(d) The Buddhists have achieved higher educational status, which has helped them to get high skilled jobs.

(e) The representation of the women Buddhists in the higher education slot is significant.

(f) There has been diversity in the occupations practised by the women Buddhists in Mumbai. Fashion designing, interior designing, advertising, etc., are some important challenging fields of occupation.

(g) Among the selected Buddhists, the majority of them are either business executives or are involved in information technology jobs.

(h) Even teachers, lecturers, doctors, engineers and advocates can be seen among the selected Buddhists in Mumbai.

(i) In all the types of higher education and occupations, women Buddhists are sharing a significant place.

(j) The income status of the selected Buddhists has been high. Majority of the selected Buddhists are earning an annual income between Rs 1,50,001 to Rs 2,00,000.

(k) All the selected Buddhists in Mumbai have accepted the culture of Buddhism.

(l) The higher educated Buddhists in Mumbai have established the unique model of development, which is based on the Ambedkarism.

(m) The model of development of the Buddhists can inspire the other Buddhists too, who are living in poverty. This model can also inspire the other backward castes.

(n) As a whole, the selected Buddhists have espoused the thoughts of Ambedkar. They have converted to Buddhism and their social identity is the result of Ambedkarism.

## References

Jadhav, Praveen (2008), *Ambedkar's People in India*, Rajat Publication, New Delhi.

Kantowsky, Dentlief (2003), *Buddhists in India Today: Description, Pictures and Documents*, Manohar Publication, New Delhi.

Wankhede, G.G. (2001), "Educational Inequalities among Scheduled Castes in Maharashtra", *EPW,* May 5.

# Chapter 7

# Ambedkarites' Socio-Political Culture

Babasaheb Ambedkar (1897–1956) had a rare dynamic persona. He also fought against a strong system all through his life. He fought a long battle against the Hindu caste system to achieve equality and freedom for Dalits in the society. He had organized a number of agitations, delivered speeches and arranged meets for the development of the untouchables in India. He had remained busy in these activities for about thirty years. Ambedkar was a great social revolutionary. He also represented the poor farmers, workers and women on different issues. And, he was a nationalist too.

The scholars ranging from academics to politics, finance to religion, have described Ambedkar as a multidimensional mind. He had been representing not only the untouchables, but also the tribes, the OBCs, the farmers, the landless labourers, the women, etc. Therefore, his contribution to the history of India is unforgettable. In the end, he also gifted Buddhism, as a new religion, to the untouchables. Unfortunately, his remarkable contribution is remembered by only the Scheduled Castes (SCs, especially the Mahars in Maharashtra) and not by the others. However, the SCs have stayed in touch with the memory and the contribution of Ambedkar for their development. In Maharashtra, the spirit of Ambedkarites can be found in a unique form. The birth anniversary (known as Ambedkar Jayanti on 14th April), the death anniversary (known as Mahaparinirvana Din on 6th December) and the conversion day (known as Dhamma Chakra Pravartana Din on 14th October) are important occasions in the life of Ambedkarites.

A number of social and political groups have participated in Ambedkarites' movement, and each one is claiming their importance. But, none of them can establish their place without the name of Ambedkar. In every function, private or public, the speech is started by paying a tribute to Ambedkar. Very few leaders have been following the ideology of Ambedkar, but they have been taking his name with pride. They have been doing this, because, the magic in the name of Ambedkar is still alive. Each leader wants to attract the Ambedkarites towards his own group in the name of Ambedkar. Most of the leaders have been promoting sentimental movement. Instead of following the thoughts and ideology of Ambedkar, they want to catch the sentiments of the Ambedkarites. The magic in the name of Ambedkar can be experienced at three important occasions mentioned above. On these occasions, all the followers of Ambedkar get united for a number of programmes. On the first occasion, Ambedkarites hold a big celebration at local level, in each village and in each town of India, especially in Maharashtra. On the second occasion, lakhs of people from all parts of Maharashtra and India arrive at Nagpur. And, on the third occasion, huge number of people arrive at Chaityabhoomi, Mumbai. The last two occasions are the most important for the political leaders, since all the Ambedkarites can be found at one place. On these occasions, each group wants to hold either a meet or a rally. The Ambedkarites may not believe in any of the present day leaders, but they do strongly believe in Ambedkar and his work. The political leaders of Ambedkarite movement have been encashing on the popularity of Ambedkar even in the twenty-first century. The spirit of the people and the magic in the name of Ambedkar can be seen on different occasions.

The socio-political activities of Ambedkar have been remarkable, which have benefited the Indian society, especially, the SCs, STs and OBCs. The agitation and fight of Ambedkar was against the social inequality created by the Hindu caste system. His speeches, writings and activities helped establish a special branch of thought, which has been known as Ambedkarism. Many times the question arises that What is Ambedkarism? Naik says that, 'A rational view of Buddhism is Ambedkarism' (2003: 43). Whereas, Sada explains it as 'democratic humanism' (1992: 99). The Ambedkarism can be traced in the preamble of the Indian Constitution, which talks about 'Justice, Liberty and Equality' in social, economic and political fields. Naik further says that, 'there has been spread of Ambedkarism in the world. The countries like Sri Lanka, Burma, Nepal, Japan, United Kingdom, America, Canada, etc. are focussing towards Ambedkarism' (2003: 44–46). 'Ambedkarism has been the focus of research in many universities and among academicians of the world'. Another scholar Nimbalkar writes that 'Ambedkarism includes equality, freedom, brotherhood and justice. Ambedkarism refuses the existence of soul, supernatural power and blind faith. Ambedkarism opposes the social inequality and slavery. Ambedkarism is based on rationalism' (1990: 13). Therefore, it can be said that Ambedkarism is a philosophy, which is most useful for the development of the society. In case of the Indian society, where the stratification has been done on the basis of caste system, Ambedkarism has a singular significance. It benefits the large majority of the society.

Mathew (1991: 135–136) explains the meaning of Ambedkarism according to the ideals and principles of Ambedkar. These are:

- Social organization should be based on the recognition of essential equality of all human beings.
- Human beings are not meant for religion but religion is meant for the human beings.
- If morality is based on the fear of God and desire for Moksha or salvation, it has no meaning; it should be based on the inner urge, without any fear or desire for reward.
- The Hindu religion, based on graded inequality, aversion and hatred for human beings, is not a religion worth the name.
- Equality, liberty and fraternity should be the aim of every society.
- One man, one value is the essence of democracy and adherence to this principle in the political spheres alone renders the democratic process complete. Realization of this aim in the real sense would mean the application of the principle in all spheres – political, economic, social, cultural and spiritual.
- Achievement of the democratic objective of one man, one value could be through peaceful and constitutional means.
- Capitalism and Brahminism are the twin enemies of Indian society and the answer is socialism and Buddhism.

- All nationalities and communities have the basic democratic right to self-determination; while the nationalities have the right to secede, the communities have the right to insurrection.

According to Thomas Mathew (ibid.), Ambedkarism is based on humanism. Therefore, it is most important for the society, especially the society where inhuman stratification exists. Ambedkarism can develop the society. Chalam (1993) has explained the relevance of Ambedkarism in contemporary India. He writes that 'Ambedkarism is an ideology, interestingly, the founder of the ideology is not Ambedkar, but his guru Mahatma Jyoti Rao Phoole. Ambedkar has developed this ideology to its logical perspective and has created an awareness among the masses and the intellectuals that the caste and casteism are the real enemies of the people. When we are referring to Ambedkarism as an ideology, we must remember that it should possess a system of political, legal, cultural, social and philosophical views and ideas that influence a whole group or national culture. The attributes of Ambedkarism are many, but the principal attribute is that it is an ideology that fights against hierarchically-based socio-economic order'. Chalam has edited the ideas of Ambedkar on the aspects of social, economic, political, philosophical, legal, research, etc., and they are relevant even today. Therefore, the ideas based on Ambedkarism can promote all the weaker sections of the society.

## Ambedkarite Movement in Maharashtra

Ambedkar established Independent Labour Party in 1936, which got tremendous success in the elections. His party served for the development of agriculturists, industrial labourers and the untouchables. In the later phase,

Ambedkar established Scheduled Castes Federation in 1942. Through this federation, he started to fight for the equality and freedom for the untouchables. Ambedkar had wanted to create a new political party named Republican Party, but due to his sad demise, he could not do so. However, the followers of Ambedkar established Republican Party of India in 1957. But, this was not a party as envisioned by Ambedkar. It was a political party of the Mahars. Dadasaheb Gaikwad, B.C. Kamble, Khobragade and others were carrying forward the Ambedkarite movement. They were able to establish its popularity to some. But, after 1964–65, the party split for a number of reasons. Some of its leaders joined the Congress party. The Ambedkarite movement lost its strength. The Ambedkarite community was divided into a number of groups and ran into problems (Nimbalkar, 1990: 63–65). The Ambedkarite community was without a strong leader. Meanwhile, a strong political organization called Dalit Panthers was established by Raja Dhale, Namdev Dhasal and others, which won great popularity among the Ambedkarites.

Ambedkarite movement in Maharashtra had been strong in the 1970s. The movement was monitored by Dalit Panthers. It was a result of the increasing serious atrocities against the Dalits in Maharashtra that Dalit Panthers was established in 1972. Raja Dhale and Namdev Dhasal, these two leaders enjoyed popularity among the SCs in Maharashtra. The whole movement was captured by the Panthers. The Dalit Panthers protested against the silver jubilee of India's independence by calling it a Black Day (in 1972). This organization was banned during emergency for demonstration of revolt (Naik, 2003: 354). This organization opposed the social injustice and atrocities with an aggressive and violent agitation. This organization created enthusiastic environment among the SCs. J.V. Pawar, Arjun Kasabe, Vijay Girkar and others were also associated with the Panthers. The Dalit Panthers had a mass base in the society. But unfortunately, the first split among the Panthers took place in 1974, and since then number of splits have taken place. Namdev Dhasal and Raja Dhale had differences between them which led to the end of this mass-based organization. Ultimately, in the year 1989, the Dalit Panthers was dissolved and absorbed in the Republican Party (Jadhav, 2000: 72–73).

Nimbalkar (1990) has explained the popularity, achievements and drawbacks of the Dalit Panthers in Maharashtra as follows: 'The branches of Dalit Panthers were being established in all the towns and villages of Maharashtra. The large majority of the Dalit youths were attracted towards this organization. Since the leaders of the organization were creating the literature, the flame of the movement went up. It was a complete unity of the Dalit leaders, which gave a big blow to the established society. The speeches of the Panthers were aggressive and attractive. The activists were reacting at every atrocity in every village and were conducting strong agitation. The best achievement of the Dalit Panthers was renaming the Marathwada University as Babasaheb Ambedkar Marathwada University. This organization was a real mass based organization in Maharashtra. But the activists of the Panthers were disciplined. They had no perfect social goal. They were lacking maturity. They believed in violence. Hence they were framed by the police department. Number of cases were registered on the names of Panthers, they were sent to the prison. Some of them were killed. Ultimately, the Dalit Panthers went for a first split in 1974 and continued with number of splits' (1990: 30–32).

Even now, the period of the Dalit Panthers is remembered by the Ambedkarites. Ambedkar had never supported violent agitation and he believed in democratic agitation. Some of the scholars have criticized the way of Panthers. But, it is a fact that there was strong social unity among the Ambedkarites. In the present time, the existence of Dalit Panthers organization is almost negligible. Namdev Dhasal holds this group of Panthers,. but the organization has no mass base.

In the contemporary period, the Ambedkarite movement has been monitored by a number of Republican Parties, but in general, there are four strong major groups or parties of Republicans, which hold the movement. They are: Republican Party of India (Athavale), Republican Party of India (Gavai), People's Republican Party of India (Kawade) and Republican Party of India-Bahujan Mahasangh (Prakash Ambedkar). The first group of Ramdas Athavale has a coalition with the Nationalistic Congress Party of Sharad Pawar, the second group of R.S. Gavai has attachment with the Congress, whereas, the third group of Jogendra Kawade and the fourth group of Prakash Ambedkar operate the movement independently. None of the leaders have got strong mass base. Comparatively, Prakash Ambedkar has been monitoring the movement with a wide vision of the backward castes. Coincidently, he happens to be the grandson of Babasaheb Ambedkar, hence this has been an important factor in monitoring the Ambedkarite movement. It must be stated that Prakash Ambedkar is an intellectual and mature leader of the Ambedkarite movement. However, he could not get a strong political success in Maharashtra. None of the leaders have enjoyed strong political success independently in Maharashtra. This has been a major limitation of the Ambedkarite movement. Apart from these, there have been a number of small political groups established at the local level. During the last few years, the political parties like Bahujan Samajwadi Party (Kashiram and Mayawati), Lokjan Shakti Party (Ramvilas Paswan) and others have also entered in Maharashtra to contain the Ambedkarite community. Although, so far, they could not establish their place among the Ambedkarites, but they have been able to give an alternative way. In the crowd of these political groups, the Ambedkarite movement has lost its political strength. Therefore, an insignificant number of Ambedkarites also have joined Congress, Nationalist Congress Party, Bharatiya Janata Party and Shiv Sena. The movement has veered towards a confused environment. Ambedkarite community has been divided into a number of groups and each group differs from others. There has been absence of unity over the ideology. Interestingly, all the political leaders from Ambedkarite community always address the meet or any function with the name of Babasaheb Ambedkar. There has been one shortcoming of the Republicans, i.e., although there have been a number of groups in the Ambedkarite movement, but these have been confined among the Mahars or the neo-Buddhists. It is a fact to some extent. It is also a fact that the Ambedkarites have been fighting for a number of social and economic problems of the SCs and the fruits have been enjoyed by all the segments of the SCs.

## Dalit Literature

The Dalit literature created by the Ambedkarites has been popular in India, especially in Maharashtra. The reason for the popularity of the Dalit Panthers organization was that their leaders like Namdev Dhasal, Raja Dhale and others were writers. This branch of literature throws a light on the social life of untouchables in India. The writers demand an aggressive change in their social situation. The writing was done in Marathi, the regional language of Maharashtra. Some of the well-known writers are Namdev Dhasal, Raja Dhale, Gangadhar Pantavane, Shankarrao Kharat, Daya Pawar, Narayan Surve and others. The Dalit literature has been so powerful that it has crossed the region of Maharashtra and even India. A number of translations of Marathi Dalit literature have been carried out in various Indian languages like Kannada, Gujarati, etc. Not only that, the literature also has been translated into English. The English writers like Eleanor Zelliot, Milton Israel, Gunther Sontheimer, etc., have translated the Dalit literature (Naik, 2003: 365–366). Interestingly, this literature has been greatly acclaimed.

Avinash Dolas (1995: 9–11), an eminent scholar of Ambedkarite movement in Maharashtra, has reviewed the Marathi Dalit literature. He writes that, 'The Dalit literature began from Ambedkarite movement. The movement could establish enthusiastic environment and a new approach among the Dalits. The beginning was as back as in 1927. The speeches of Ambedkar were presented by the artists in the form of poems and stories. Number of newspapers and journals were started and through which various writers were putting their views towards the Dalits'. The present author has reviewed the Dalit literature created by Anna Bhau Sathe *(Fakira)*, Shankarrao Kharat *(Manuskichi Haak)*, Sukharam Hivarale *(Gaavkari)*, Baburao Bagal *(Jevha Mee Jaat Chorali)*, Vaman Hoval *(Benayad)* and others. Dolas also says that some of the writers from the upper castes, like V.M. Joshi, Mama Varekar, V.S. Khandekar, Kolhatkar and others were inspired by Gandhi's philosophy, whereas, some of the writers (from the upper castes) like V.V. Shirvadkar, Anant Kanekar, Karandikar, Bedekar and other were inspired by Marx's philosophy. But, the writers from the panthers and others from the Dalit community have created anti-Hindu social literature. He further points out that, 'During 1970–1980, the Dalit literature was dominated by the writers from the wing of Dalit Panthers. Namdev Dhasal, Raja Dhale, J.V. Pawar, Arjun Dangle, Avinash Mahatekar and others had created an appealing literature in the form of poems and stories, which attracted the Dalit youths' (Dolas, 1995: 58–59).

## Conclusion

The Ambedkarites' socio-political movement and culture has been based on Ambedkarism. There has definitely been a contribution of all the Republican leaders in the post-Ambedkar period. They have tried their best to transfer the Ambedkarites' culture to the next generation. They also have created social awareness among the Ambedkrites. However, in recent times, they have not been united. As a result, their movement is not united. The Republican Party of India has split into various groups. They have lost their political power. They are also losing their control over the masses. The established and powerful parties are using them. Besides the political power in the contemporary period, the Ambedkarites' socio-political culture after 1956 seems to be positive.

## References

Chalam, K.S. (1993) (ed.), *Relevance of Ambedkarism in India*, Rawat Publications, New Delhi, Jaipur.

Dolas, Avinash (1995), *Marathi Dalit Katha*, Savita Prakashan, Aurangabad (in Marathi).

Jadhav, Raja (2000), *Saha December 1956 and Nantar*, Granthali Prakashan, Mumbai (in Marathi).

Naik, C.D. (2003), *Thoughts and Philosophy of Dr B.R. Ambedkar*, Sarup & Sons Publication, New Delhi (in Marathi).

Nimbalkar (1990), *Ambedkari Vicharanchi Disha*, Prabodhan Prakashan, Nagpur (in Marathi).

Sada, Karhade (1992), *Marxwad, Buddhawad Aani Ambedkarwad*, Granthali Prakashan, Mumbai (in Marathi).

# Chapter 8

# Ambedkarites' Tributes to Chaityabhoomi

Every year on 6th December, on the occasion of Ambedkar's death anniversary or Mahaparinirvana Day of Ambedkar, lakhs of people from all parts of Maharashtra and India visit the Chaityabhoomi to pay a tribute to their great leader. The people are so much devoted that for the last 48 years they have been consistently paying their tribute to the memory of Ambedkar. This tremendous response of the people shows that there is/was no other leader, academician and political, social reformer as popular as Ambedkar. It is only the name of Ambedkar that brings the large assembly of people to the Chaityabhoomi. The gathering of Ambedkarites at the Chaityabhoomi has been an attraction for the researchers. Hence, we too had conducted a field survey in order to analyse the general mindset of Ambedkarites at Chaityabhoomi. The following analysis has been given on the basis of field survey conducted on 6th December 2004, i.e., on the 48th death anniversary of Ambedkar. The given analysis is based on the observation method.

In order to understand the importance of Chaityabhoomi, it is essential to explain the location and the background of the fieldwork. Since the Chaityabhoomi is located at Dadar, Mumbai, we are giving a brief information about the location, starting from Maharashtra to the Chaityabhoomi. Maharashtra state is located in western India, bounded on the north by Madhya Pradesh, in the south by Andhra Pradesh, Karnataka and Goa, and on the west by the Arabian Sea and northeast by Daman and Gujarat. The state has an area of 3,07,713 sq km. Population of Maharashtra in 2001 was 9,67,52,247. The area of Greater Bombay is 603 sq km with a population of about 16.4 million. Bombay or Mumbai is located in the north-west of Maharashtra state (Turner, 2005: 811–817).

The islands that now form Mumbai were first home to the Koli fisherfolk as far back as the 2nd century BC. The islands were ruled by the succession of Hindu dynasties from the 6th century AD, invaded by Muslims in the 14th century and then ceded to Portugal by the Sultan of Gujarat in 1534. The Portuguese did little to develop them before the major island of the group was included in Catherine of Braganza's dowry, when she married England's Charles II in 1661. The British took possession of the islands in 1665. Then called Bombay, the area soon developed as a trading port and merchants were attracted from all parts. Within 20 years, the presidency of East India Company was transferred to Bombay from Surat and it became the trading headquarters for the whole west coast of India (Singh, 2003: 736–737).

Bombay played a formative role in the struggle for independence, hosting the first Indian National Congress in 1885 and the launch of the Quit India campaign in 1942. After the independence, the city became the capital of the Bombay Presidency. In 1960, this presidency was divided on the linguistic grounds into Maharashtra and Gujarat. Bombay then became the capital of Marathi-speaking

Maharashtra (ibid., 737–738). Very recently, Bombay has been renamed as Mumbai. Mumbai has a number of tourist places, namely, Tajmahal Hotel, Kala Ghoda, Chhatrapati Shivaji Terminus, Bombay University, Chowpatty, Gateway of India, etc. One such location within Mumbai is Dadar.

This location can be understood clearly through the railway network. There are two train systems being operated out of Mumbai. Central Railways handles services to the east and the south plus a few trains to the north. It operates from the Chhatrapati Shivaji Terminus (CST). A few Central Railways depart from Dadar, a few stations north of CST. The other train system is Western Railways, which provides services to the north (India) from Mumbai Central. Mumbai has an efficient but overcrowded suburban train network. There are three main lines, making it easy to navigate. One is from Churchgate heading north to stations such as Charni Road, Mahalaxmi, Vile Parle, etc. A couple of the other suburban lines operate from CST servicing places such as Byculla, Dadar, Neral, etc. Few trains also operate from Dadar, which is an important destination for changing the train route.

The area of Mumbai is about 437.77 sq km, comprising a population of about 20 million (for Mumbai metropolitan area, Thane and Navi Mumbai). The geographical location is: latitude 18°53' north, longitude 72°50' east. Mumbai's temperatures are stable. The city has a warm and humid climate throughout the year. Regional language of Mumbai is Marathi, however English, Hindi, Gujarati are also spoken in the city. Majority of the people speak Hindi, about a half speak Marathi and a quarter Gujarati. Local trains, buses, taxis and autorickshaws are the major means of public transport in Mumbai. Local trains operate on three lines, i.e., western, central and harbour. For the convenience of the commuters, monthly and quarterly passes are also made available. Brihan Mumbai Electricity Supply and Transport (BEST) buses cover almost all of Mumbai and are linked to all the suburban railway stations. Air-conditioned/luxury services are also available on select routes. Taxis ply all over the city and its suburbs. Mumbai is a shopper's paradise. It has every kind of product, in every price range, to suit every wallet. Shops could be found in the streets and at Crawford Market, Colaba Causeway, Fashion Street, World Trade Centre, Breach Candy, Linking Road and Dadar, etc.

Dadar is a place known well for its markets. Dadar railway station is a junction and hence, it has its own significance. The Chaityabhoomi, the place where Ambedkar was cremated, is located 2 kms away from the Dadar Railway Station in the west. It is situated next to Shivaji Park, one famous place of Dadar. The Chaityabhoomi is located on the banks of Arabian Sea. The Chaityabhoomi, a place where Ambedkar was cremated, has been an important place for the followers of Ambedkar. On the occasion of his 48th death anniversary, lakhs of people had visited this place. This was a great gathering. We could get some of the observations of the people at Chaityabhoomi as noted below:

## Ambedkarites' Tribute: Nature and Activities

The Ambedkarites have been offering tribute to their leader on different occasions. His death anniversary has been an important day for them. On this day, the Ambedkarites from all the parts of Maharashtra and India come to Chaityabhoomi, Mumbai to offer their tribute. We have tried to explain here the nature of the tribute and the activities of the Ambedkarites.

### *From Dadar to Chaityabhoomi*

Dadar railway station has been an important destination for people who travel by trains. It is the nearest railway station to reach the Chaityabhoomi. Therefore, Dadar station was also important for the followers of Ambedkar, in order to reach the Chaityabhoomi and to pay tribute to Ambedkar. The surrounding environment at Dadar station on 6th December every year has been similar. On 6th December 2004, the Dadar station was overflowing with the Ambedkarites. The trains coming from all the parts of Maharashtra and India, generally, make a stop at Dadar. Ambedkarites were arriving at Dadar station from every train. Large number of people had arrived from the night of 5th December to the morning of 6th December 2004. The people, especially, who had to cross a long distance were coming by the trains, e.g., from Nagpur, Yavatmal, Kolhapur, Sangli, Solapur, etc., and from outside Maharashtra. The people residing nearby Mumbai, Thane, Pune, etc., were arriving by private vehicles and state transport buses. Dadar station was over packed by the people. The people were wearing either blue caps or blue badges or blue clothes. The blue colour is a symbol of Ambedkarites. Some people had blue flags. All the platforms at Dadar station were overflowing. The people were moving towards the overbridge, which connects the Chaityabhoomi road. The overbridge had two main gates/sides, one was in the east and second was in west. The people were moving towards the west side, which connects the Chaityabhoomi. The distance between Dadar station to Chaityabhoomi was about 2 kms. The road looked blue and there was so much crowd that hardly any vehicle could pass. Single person, couples, children, the old, families and all types of people were going by the road. All of them had a common objective of paying tribute to Ambedkar. While walking towards the Chaityabhoomi, no one was found either busy in shopping or eating. However, the people coming back to Dadar station after paying tribute were busy in either shopping or eating. This shows that the Ambedkarites' first priority was to pay tribute to Ambedkar. Such is their commitment and spirit on that day. After paying the tribute, they were satisfied. This explains the love of the people towards their great leader. This intense love or spirit is alive even after 48 years of the death of Ambedkar. Ambedkar was a real leader of the masses. The road to Chaityabhoomi goes through Kabootarkhana, a place on this road. At this place, there is a slight turn in the right direction and then it is straight.

The road to Chaityabhoomi is simple. All the flow of the people was going in the same direction. Some of the Ambedkarites were coming for the first time to visit the Chaityabhoomi. But, they had no problem in ascertaining the location. Only thing they had to do, was to follow the next group of people. It seemed as if all the people and the roads converged at Chaityabhoomi. It was 8 a.m. There were volunteers at every corner of the road. They were deputed by the Buddhist Society of India. The volunteers were guiding the people and also managing the traffic on select corners. All the volunteers were wearing blue caps. The volunteers were found on Savarkar Road, Ranade Road, Shivaji Park and Prabhadevi. By all these roads, Ambedkarites were coming to Chaityabhoomi.

We observed a large number of Ambedkarites, who were either aged or physically handicapped. The aged were associated with their sons or family. They were walking with strong commitment and spirit which could be seen on their faces. It was the power of Ambedkar's thought. It was their love for Ambedkar. The researcher came across a number of physically disabled persons and had conversation with one blind couple. The blind couple was being assisted with one other person, who was their relative. This was their third visit on 6th December. This also evinces the same commitment and spirit. Other physically disabled persons, were either on wheel chairs or with hand sticks or with other family members. The rally ultimately reached the Chaityabhoomi, where we found a mega queue. The queue was lined on one side of the road. People were either joining the queue or staying at the open place by the sea.

### *Queue at Chaityabhoomi*

The people were standing in the queue since the late night of 5th December 2004. The queue was very systematic and disciplined. No one was trying to break the queue. The length of the queue was about 5 kms (approximately). We found this situation at 9 a.m. on 6th December 2004. As the time was passing, the queue was lengthening. The Chaityabhoomi was opened at 4 a.m. All the people were quiet and calm. They were not in a hurry. They were shouting slogans like Jai Bhim, Ambedkarancha Vijaya Aso, Ambedkar Amar Rahe. This was giving energy to them to stay in the queue without feeling tired. On an average, everyone had to stay at least for around 5–6 hours in the queue. Yet, they remained enthusiastic. At one corner of the queue was Chaityabhoomi and the second corner had crossed Prabhadevi, an important place near Dadar. The queue had a zigzag shape at some places, crossing through Shivaji Park, Century Bazaar, etc. There were a number of volunteers and police in order to control the situation. No one disturbed the peace at Chaityabhoomi. Many people went directly towards the open space near the sea, which is located on the one side of Chaityabhoomi. They were paying tribute from that place. However, the calm of the queue at Chaityabhoomi was very surprising. It was not a queue outside the temple, but a queue to pay tribute to a great man, Ambedkar. Therefore, the queue was significant and unique.

### *People at Chaityabhoomi*

This was the 48th death anniversary of Ambedkar. The area from Chaityabhoomi, Shivaji Park to Dadar was occupied by Ambedkarites. The flow of the people was so much high that it was like a competition in which, on one side, it was the Arabian Sea and on second side, the blue sea of Ambedkarites. There was a huge pandal on Shivaji Park ground for the people. Number of newspapers had estimated the strength of the Ambedkarites at Chaityabhoomi. *Mumbai Sandhya* (6th December 2004, p. 1 and 4, an evening daily published from Mumbai) had reported that the strength of the people at Chaityabhoomi was about 25 lakhs. Another daily from Mumbai, i.e., *Samrat* (7th December 2004, front page) had estimated the strength as 20 lakhs. Another daily, *Loksatta* (7th December 2004, p. 2) had reported that 25 lakhs of people had arrived at Chaityabhoomi on 6th December 2004, to pay tribute to Ambedkar. The enthusiasm of the Ambedkarites at Chaityabhoomi was really surprising. This was an overwhelming response and their love for Ambedkar. After paying tribute to Ambedkar, the people were moving towards the sea. Some of them were enjoying boating and some of them were going to the sea front. The people at the Chaityabhoomi were now tired. Most of them had travelled without sleep, yet, they were looking fresh. The people at Chaityabhoomi represented the power and spirit of the Ambedkarite movement. After arriving at Chaityabhoomi, the first commitment was to pay tribute to Ambedkar. The preparation of the people showed that the death anniversary of Ambedkar has been an important day for the followers of Ambedkar.

## Organizations/Institutions at Service

Every year lakhs of Ambedkarites visit Chaityabhoomi. Since the people come from all the parts of Maharashtra and India, they need a number of facilities or services. The Municipal Corporation of Mumbai has been performing its duty for a number of years, but it has limitations regarding extending the services to the people. The Corporation has been providing very few services like cleaning, sanitation, medical and a few others. In comparison to the size of the population, these services seemed to be very negligible. Therefore, depending on the services of Corporation was not feasible. A number of social, political and cultural organizations of Ambedkarites have been providing all types of services at Chaityabhoomi. In order to manage the people and to provide a number of services to the people, number of organizations/institutions have planned arrangements. The giant responsibility is shared by the Buddhist Society of India. The chairman of the society Meeratai Ambedkar and other officers were monitoring the services at Chaityabhoomi. The Buddhist Society of India has been rendering the services for several years. On this day, the society had a proper planning as follows:

The Buddhist Society of India had classified the Chaityabhoomi and surrounding area in 11 parts. Each part had been monitored by its volunteers. All the arrangements had been done to manage the the crowd of people and to maintain the discipline. All the classified parts were monitored by the officers and volunteers of the society. The Buddhist Society of India had deputed its volunteers in large numbers. Fifteen assistant-chiefs, 40 officers, 3,300 volunteers and 2,000 volunteers of Samata Sainik Dal were deputed. In some parts, the society had taken the help of local organizations. Above all, a special squad also had been deputed for emergency service. Along with the society, there were around 200 local organizations and mandals. The lady volunteers were also in significant number. Some of the responsible officers were: S.K. Bhandare, B.H. Gaikwad, Maruti Sarode, N.M. Agane, Jagadish Gavai, D.D. Kasabe, D.T. Sonavane, Sushma Tai Pawar, Shashikala Balakhande, Anant Jadhav, B.K. Ahire and others (*Samrat*, 3rd November 2004).

Mumbai Municipal Corporation had arranged sanitation services for the people arriving at Chaityabhoomi. A mega pandal had been created, where 6,000 people could rest. The pandal was constructed at Shivaji Park, Mumbai. Several other organizations and political parties had established stalls at Chaityabhoomi. Each one was trying to contribute or to help in some or the other way. Meal service, medical service, drinking water service, information about Human Rights and other types of services were provided free of cost. Some of the organizations which had established their stalls at Chaityabhoomi were: All India SC/ST Railway Employees Association, Central Railway, Matunga, Mumbai, Ramai Utkarsha Sangh, Oriental Bank of Commerce SC/ST Employees Welfare Association (Maharashtra Zone), Sanghamitra Backward Cooperative Credit Society, Mauli Charitable, Medical Trust, the Republican Party of India (Athavale), Bahujan Vidyarthi Parishad, Ambedkar Centre for Justice and Peace, etc. There were a number of book shops, cassette stalls and photo stalls. Police officials had been deputed in sufficient numbers with police vans. The stalls of the organizations could be seen on all the roads leading to Chaityabhoomi. Every organization was rendering the service for the followers of Ambedkar with honesty. In a collective way, it was the unity of all the Ambedkarites at Chaityabhoomi. The 48th Mahaparinirvana Din or the death anniversary of Ambedkar was a big occasion.

### *Meal Service*

The meal was the most essential service of the Ambedkarites at Chaityabhoomi. The people had travelled for one or two days before 6th December 2004. Large majority of them were poor and could not spend money in the hotels. Therefore, the people were in need of a meal. To provide meal service at Chaityabhoomi, a number of arrangements had been made. On the occasion of the 48th death anniversary of Ambedkar, various organizations had arranged free breakfast and meal service at Chaityabhoomi. A number of stalls to provide meal service were established around Chaityabhoomi. There was a long queue of Ambedkarites outside the stall to get this service. This service was made available on the 5th and 6th December of 2004. Some of the organizations, which had provided the meal service at Chaityabhoomi, were as follows: All India SC/ST Railway Employees Association, Central Railway, Matunga, Mumbai, etc., had established their stalls through which the distribution of meal to the people was carried out. Ramai Utkarsha Sangh also organized a free meal service for the people. Oriental Bank of Commerce SC/ST Employees Welfare Association (Maharashtra Zone) also had established a stall where the meal had been distributed among the people free of cost. Shivshakti Social Organization also had distributed a free meal among the people.

On the occasion of the 48th death anniversary of Ambedkar, the large number of Bhikus had arrived at

Chaityabhoomi from Uttar Pradesh, Madhya Pradesh, Bihar and Delhi. The Municipal Corporation of Mumbai had arranged the lodging facilities. The Vichar Probodhan Manch of Bhandup had arranged the meal service for the Bhikus on the 5th and 6th December 2004 (*Samrat*, 13th December 2004, p. 3).

The Republican Party of India (Athavale), Bahujan Vidyarthi Parishad and several other organizations had provided the free meal service at Chaityabhoomi. Ambedkarites could be seen waiting in the long queues outside every meal stall. All of them were disciplined. No one was trying to cross the line. The organisers were busy in performing the activities. All of the organisers were sincere in their work. All the followers of Ambedkar were taking the meal after paying tribute to Ambedkar at Chaityabhoomi.

### *Drinking Water Facility*

One of the most essential facility required by the Ambedkarites after arriving at Chaityabhoomi was of the drinking water. Since people had no personal arrangements, it was an important service. A number of organizations were providing the drinking water facility. Some of them could be named here. The Central Excise Department's employees had arranged this facility for the people. Similar kind of service was also made available by the Buddhist Insurance Employees Welfare Organization and Life Insurance Corporation of India. This facility was made available on 5th and 6th December 2004. The drinking water was made available at every distance of 60–70 metres. A number of organizations had organized such facility. There were sufficient number of people who availed of this facility.

### *Medical Facilities*

The Ambedkarites coming from the rural area always lacked medical facilities. There are two reasons for this, one – the rural area lacks medical facilities, and two – the poor Ambedkarites cannot afford this service. Most of the people do not go for a proper medical check-up. Therefore, the medical facilities have been an important part of the services being provided at Chaityabhoomi. Hence, for the benefit of the Ambedkarites, a number of social, political and cultural organizations had arranged free medical facilities for the people at Chaityabhoomi. The Buddhist Society of India had established a medical centre, where free medical help had been provided. The main content of the medical facilities was the free check-up of eyes and free distribution of spectacles. This facility was made available on the 5th and 6th December of 2004. At this centre, about 2,500 people were given medical help and about 1,000 people were given free spectacles. The centre had a group of doctors, which included Dr Supriya Dalavi, Dr Sharad Savant, Dr Vidya Mane, Dr More, Dr Sushma Survade, Dr Hemangi Balakhande and others. The chairman of the society, Meeratai Ambedkar had visited the centre to monitor the situation. Ambedkarites were waiting in a long queue to get this facility. Sanghamitra Backward Cooperative Credit Society and Mauli Charitable Medical Trust had provided a free distribution of spectacles and free health care facilities (*Samrat*, 9th December 2004).

All India Bank of Maharashtra SC/ST Employees Association also had organized free medical facilities at Chaityabhoomi. The Municipal Corporation of Mumbai and several other organizations also had organized centres, where free medical facilities were made available. The response of the people was overwhelming. Large majority of the people had benefited by this facility. Majority of the beneficiaries had a rural background.

### *Awareness of Human Rights*

The Ambedkarites have been lacking the awareness about the human rights. The increasing atrocities have been a serious problem in India. Many times, the people do not have the knowledge about the rights. Once the rights are known to the people, they can fight for that. This type of service is essential throughout the life of the people. There is one special organization, which has been fighting for the social justice for the Ambedkarites and has created a centre of awareness at Chaityabhoomi. Ambedkar Centre for Justice and Peace, an organization located at Mumbai, had established a special stall or centre at Chaityabhoomi. The objective of the organization was to create awareness about the human rights among Ambedkarites. The stall of human rights was inaugurated by Uddhav Kamble, an IPS officer. At this stall, advice on human rights protection and education was given to the people free of cost. The whole exercise was monitored by Mrs Vandana Aparanti. The large majority of urban-centric people had visited the stall. This stall was unique, since this was imparting the knowledge about the rights of the Ambedkarites. There have been increasing cases of atrocities in India. In this position, such awareness definitely helps.

### *Cleaning the Area Around Chaityabhoomi*

Since Chaityabhoomi is located at the Dadar Chowpatty, the sea side at Mumbai, everyday thousands of people from all parts of Mumbai, Maharashtra and India have been visiting Chowpatty to enjoy the beauty of the sea. Therefore, huge garbage and uncleanliness can be found there on any day.

The Mahaparinirvana Din of Ambedkar has been a major event for Ambedkarites and lakhs of people have been visiting the Chaityabhoomi, so it is very essential to clean the surrounding area of Chaityabhoomi. The cleaning activities are generally carried out by the Corporation. On the occasion of the 48th death anniversary of Ambedkar, the Municipal Corporation of Mumbai had deputed its employees at Chaityabhoomi to clean the area. Along with this, several other organizations also had participated in the cleaning activities. The cleaning activities were continued even after the occasion. In this regard, Sanjivini Pratishthan had carried out the cleaning activities at Chaityabhoomi on 6th and 7th December 2004. This was a civic responsibility accepted by the organization.

## *Bookstalls*

The Marathi literature has thrown much light on the social life of the Dalits. Some of the writers were of the higher castes, who have created the dalit characters on the basis of communist philosophy. However, after 1970, there have been an increasing number of literary work on the Dalits. Interesting thing of it is that, they belong to the Dalit community. Rather, the Ambedkarite movement has been moving through the creation of Dalit literature or Ambedkarite literature. In the contemporary period, such literature has become popular among the people. The real Dalit literature has a background of Dalit Panthers. a political group established in the seventies. As per Naik, 'In the first quarter of seventies Dalit Panthers and Dalit literature in India became well known features of Dalit movement as Black Panthers and Black literature in America had been of Black Movement. In the year 1972 two Dalit writers namely, Namdev Dhasal and Raja Dhale founded Dalit organization called Dalit Panthers. Through this body, a mass protest was launched against atrocities on untouchables and Buddhists in Maharashtra' (2003: 357–358). It was followed by numerous works of literature. By the end of the 20th century, the Dalit literature or Ambedkarite literature was well established and gave a direction to the movement. The Ambedkarites had accepted this literature and have been responding positively. The immense response of the people towards the Ambedkarite literature could be seen at Chaityabhoomi on 6th December 2004.

On the occasion of the 48th Mahaparinirvana Day of Ambedkar, there were bookstalls at Chaityabhoomi. Publishers and the booksellers were present on the 6th December 2004. All the publishers and the booksellers dedicated to the Ambedkarite movement had gathered at Chaityabhoomi. All of them had put up the stalls in one line. There were around thirty bookstalls. English version books were also there though less in number. The response of the people towards the bookstalls was overwhelming. Every one was visiting the bookstall and purchasing one or the other book. This was really surprising in case of the Ambedkarites who live in poverty, but they were purchasing books. The maximum demand was for the books written by Ambedkar (Marathi version). Some of the books of Ambedkar have crossed about 70 years of publication, but even now, the demand for these books was quite high. Most of the people were purchasing small sized book considering the price factor. Some financially established people were purchasing bundles of books. It was well known to the Ambedkarites that on the occasion of Mahaparinirvana Din, all types of books could be available. Such response can be seen every year. More interestingly, the books on Shivaji, Sambhaji, Shahu Maharaj, etc., and the Maratha leaders also got significant response. The books written by the Maratha Seva

Sangh were also available for the sale. The overwhelming response of the Ambedkarites towards the books shows that the Dalit literature or Ambedkarite literature has been popular and has played an important role in the Ambedkarite movement.

### *Stalls of Photographs, Caps, Badges, etc.*

The Ambedkarites have created a special identity, which expresses their love and devotion towards their great leader, Ambedkar. Every household of an Ambedkarite includes at least two photos on the wall. One is, of Tathagat Gautam Buddha and another is, of Ambedkar. This is their identity and they are proud of it. When two Ambedkarites meet, they say Jay Bhim instead of Hello or Namaskar. This is the spirit of the Ambedkarites. Some of them also use caps, badges and other types of articles, which indicate the Ambedkarite movement. The Ambedkarites are always in search of special photographs of Ambedkar. Thus, the occasions like Mahaparinirvana Din are an important day for all these people.

There were stalls, which were put up at Chaityabhoomi to sell the photographs, caps, badges, name plates, etc. All these goods displayed Ambedkar. Ambedkarites were crowded at these stalls, which were selling blue caps, blue ribbons, badges, photo, etc. The blue colour is the colour of Ambedkarites. Large majority of the people were purchasing some or the other type of article. The people were wearing either a blue cap or a blue ribbon or a badge. The blue ribbon was supposed to be tied around the head. On every ribbon, Jay Bhim was printed. On the cap, at the centre, same words were printed. Some of the people were purchasing the badge on which the photo of Ambedkar was printed. The badge was supposed to be worn on the chest. The people were purchasing and wearing it happily. Once such typical ribbon or cap or badge comes on the head or chest of a person, whose spirit could be read very clearly. Every article had photographs of Ambedkar for sale. The photographs were available in all sizes. The people were looking carefully at the photographs and were purchasing them. There were also photographs of Gautam Buddha, Mahatma Phoole, Shahu Maharaj, etc. The people were responding significantly towards these photographs too. There were also steel plates on which Jay Bhim or Namo Buddhay was printed. It could be put on the doors of the house. Such plates were also available in the form of stickers.

### *Cassette Stalls*

The music has been an important part of the Ambedkarite movement. The social and political activities of Ambedkar have been presented through the songs or music. Some of the singers have been an integral part of such movement. The folk music has been appealing to the people. They have been listening to songs and music, dedicated to Ambedkar. The demand for such music has been increasing day by day, and in response the cassette companies have been producing the cassettes. Recently, the songs or music on Ambedkar also have been produced in compact disc (CD). On the occasions, which are dedicated to the Ambedkarite movement, variety of cassettes and CDs have been sold. Every year, the Ambedkarites have been purchasing a number of cassettes/CDs dedicated to Ambedkar. Keeping this demand of Ambedkarites in mind, cassette/CD sellers had opened stalls at Chaityabhoomi. Each seller had displayed a variety of music. The sound at the cassette stalls was very loud. Every cassette seller was trying to attract the people. In this exercise, there had been loud sound at Chaityabhoomi.

Actually the 6th December is a sad day for the Ambedkarites, hence some of the organizations had appealed to the sellers to keep the sound at a lower pitch. Since the awareness was created by the Buddhist Society of India, the cassette stalls were trying to maintain their sound at a low pitch. This change helped maintain the feeling of the death anniversary. There were also compact disks (CDs) in audio and video form. But, majority of the songs were in the cassette form. These songs are called Bhim Songs, i.e., the songs on Bhimrao alias Babasaheb Ambedkar. All of the songs were relating the marvellous activities of Ambedkar and Ambedkar's Buddhism. The people were asking for a variety of cassettes. Majority of them were eager to have cassettes of Vishnu Shinde. The cassette sellers were showing it by playing the cassette. The people were listening to about half of the song and were then trying to catch the rhythm by heart. The sale was going on 5th and 6th December 2004. But, 6th December was the most busy day.

### *Awareness through Folk Music*

As explained above, the music has been an integral part of the Ambedkarites movement. It has got social appeal. Therefore, a number of cultural groups have been trying to spread the message of Ambedkar through music. Among these, the folk music has been popular since it has got a catching rhythm. The cultural groups have been performing programmes all over Maharashtra on different occasions. Since the 6th December has been an important day in the life of Ambedkarites a number of cultural groups have been trying to spread the idea and message of Ambedkar through the folk music at Chaityabhoomi. On the occasion of the 48th death anniversary of Ambedkar, such organizations were at work with a social goal. Some of the local cultural groups from Mumbai and around were trying to spread the message of the work of Ambedkar through the folk music. The songs of Waman Dada Kardak and of others were sung by this group. Along with this, compositions about Ambedkar, Buddhism and its awareness were also sung. The group consisted of 5–6 members. They had limited musical instruments like harmonium and dholaki. One of them was singing. Lots of people were listening to them. Interestingly, this group was not singing for the money. They had a book, in which poems were handwritten. All of them were wearing either blue caps or blue ribbons or badges. Within a song, they had covered all the important events that had happened in the life of Ambedkar. The level of rhythm was at a higher pace. Such groups were not in large numbers. The use of 'dholaki' was maximum during the playing of songs to attract the people. The folk music being played by the cultural group could give some amount of knowledge about Ambedkar's social and political activities to the people.

### *Hoardings*

Ambedkarites in India, especially in Maharashtra, come together on such occasions. There has been perfect unity and strength of the Ambedkarites on these days. Therefore, these days are also equally important for the political parties, especially for the Republican Party. The political leaders or the Republicans get maximum exposure on these days. Hence, no one wants to miss these days. Lakhs of people visit Chaityabhoomi every year to pay tribute to Ambedkar. This has been a good opportunity for the political leaders to approach the Ambedkarites. The 6th December, i.e., the day of death anniversary of Ambedkar has been an important day for all the political leaders; hence they give themselves, maximum exposure. On 6th December, maximum exposure to the political leaders is given through hoardings or display boards. The hoardings are arranged around the

Chaityabhoomi. There are a variety of hoardings available in different sizes. Thus, on his 48th death anniversary, every political leader had tried to place his hoarding. On the hoarding or display board, on one side, the photograph of Ambedkar and on the second, the photograph of the leader appeared. Below these photographs, the name of the political party and political leader was printed in bold letters. The intention of the hoarding was to pay tribute to Ambedkar. But, the way in which the hoardings were placed, it was reflecting something different. There was a competition between the political leaders. The hoarding of Ramdas Athavale (Member of Parliament) was of large size and the photograph was showing that, 'after Ambedkar, there is no one, but Athavale'. Was Athavale trying to place himself in the place of Ambedkar? Such questions were raised in the minds of the Ambedkarites. Among all the hoardings, the hoarding of Ramdas Athavale, Balasaheb Ambedkar and Jogendra Kawade were major. Along with these, all the local leaders and various political parties also had placed their hoardings. One hoarding was about a local leader, whose photo was printed along with a gun. Although, Ambedkar had neither supported nor conducted any agitation based on violence so such a hoarding was misleading the Ambedkarites. The hoardings could be found in all the roads, which go towards Chaityabhoomi. The main intention of the hoardings should have been to express the tribute of respective leaders towards Ambedkar. But, the way in which these hoardings were placed, showed that every leader wanted to express his importance in the Ambedkarite movement.

The Ambedkarites had arrived from all the parts of Maharashtra. Nearly all of the people prefer to come by rail. On the occasion of the death anniversary, most of the people have been travelling free of cost. It is not unusual. There are a number of events organized by the Hindu organizations where every year large number of people have been travelling for such events without tickets. The events include either a rally of Hindu organization or political parties or a number of yatras in all parts of Maharashtra. Besides these, the government also has given a huge financial grant towards the Kumbh Mela. In comparison to all these, the event of Chaityabhoomi is negligible. However, on the occasion of the 48th death anniversary of Ambedkar, a large number of police force had been deputed and a strict enforcement of law was observed by the department.

After the ceremonies were over, the visitors went to Chhatrapati Shivaji Terminal (CST), an important terminal of railway at Mumbai. Some of the people remained at Dadar station. At CST, the railway police did not allow the people to move towards the railways initially. Some of the people tried to cross the police, but the police officials used lathis (sticks) to block them. All the people were forced to sit in one compact place. It was very difficult to sit comfortably. This went on till late night. The departure of the people was very troublesome. The railway administration had announced one special train to Nagpur, but it was inadequate. Many people had to stay there for the whole night. They were accompanied by children. The situation at CST was the worst. Similar situation could be found at Dadar also. Thus, the departure of Ambedkarites has been a serious problem.

### Tribute to Ambedkar by the People of Maharashtra

Ambedkar has rendered remarkable service to his people in India, especially in Maharashtra. He has sacrificed his whole life for the development of the backward castes. He made a number of constitutional provisions for the development of depressed castes. He fought against the orthodox Hindu caste system. The followers of Ambedkar never forget Ambedkar Jayanti, Dhammachakra Pravartana Din and Mahaparinirvana Din. These days are important occasions in the life of the followers of Ambedkar, especially the neo-Buddhist. In Maharashtra, a number of programmes have been organized by the people on these occasions at different levels. Those who cannot come to Chaityabhoomi, also have been paying tribute at the local level. This is a common programme among the Ambedkarites. All the political leaders, educationists, social workers and common people have been a part of this. This can be seen in all the parts of Maharashtra. Some of the select events have been described below:

**Karjat, Mumbai:** Various organizations and political parties had come together to pay tribute to Ambedkar. A huge crowd had gathered near the statue of Ambedkar, located at the central part of Karjat, to garland the statue. Republican Party of India, Bharip-Bahujan Mahasangh, Bahujan Samaj Party, Akhil Bhartiya Mahasangh, the Buddhist Society of India, BAMSEF, Sambhaji Brigade, Disha Kendra, All India SC/ST Union, Bahujan Seva Sangh and other organizations had also participated (*Samrat,* 8th December 2004, p. 6).

**Parbhani:** Programmes at different locations in Parbhani were arranged to pay tribute to Ambedkar. Sajjulala, Vijaya Varpudkar, Kumbhar and others participated. The people residing in Ajitnagar, Phule Colony, Sarnath Colony, Goutam Nagar, Santsena Nagar, Ambedkar Nagar (at Parbhani) also paid their tribute (*Samrat,* 8th December 2004, p. 6).

**Solapur:** Tributes ware paid to Ambedkar at Solapur by a number of organizations and political parties. The statue of Ambedkar situated at Park Chowk was surrounded by thousands of people. The people garlanded the statue at twelve in the night. Raja Saravade (Republican Party of India-Athavale), Gangubai Gaikwad (Bahujan Samaj Party), P.R. Bansode (Bharip Bahujan Mahasangh) and several others had garlanded the statue (*Samrat,* 10th December 2004).

**Akola:** Akhil Bharatiya Buddhagaya Mahabodhi Vihar Andolan Samiti and Akhil Bharatiya Bhikshu Mahasangh had organized a programme on Buddhism on the occasion of the 48th death anniversary of Ambedkar. This was a special programme which explained the need of Buddhism in the life of Ambedkarites (*Samrat,* 10th December 2004).

**Dharavi:** Dharavi is the biggest slum area in Mumbai. On the occasion of the death anniversary of Ambedkar, the residents of Dharavi had organized a candlelight march to pay tribute to their leader. The march began on 5th December at 11 p.m. from Prajna Buddh Vihar. All the people were saying, 'Buddham Saranam Gachchami'. Sanjay Kasare, Kiran Mohite, Suresh Jadhav and others had participated in the march (*Samrat,* 9th December 2004, p. 6).

**Kalyan:** Naresh Gaikwad Cultural Organization of Kalyan had arranged a candle march on 5th December 2004. The march began at Khadakpada and ended at Ambedkar Garden. Vivek Gaikwad, Amit Kharate, Prafull Vohal and others had organized this march (*Samrat,* 9th December 2005, p. 6).

**Vasind:** A programme was arranged by the Ambedkarites in Vasind on the occasion of the death anniversary of Ambedkar. The statue of Ambedkar was garlanded by the guest, Nalini Pandit. Sujata Nikam, Surekha Gaikwad, Sanjay Bhalerao and several others participated in the programme to pay tribute to their leader (*Samrat,* 9th December 2004, p. 6).

**Nasik:** The Ambedkarites of Nasik organized a programme of paying tribute at the statue of Ambedkar (*Samrat,* 9th December 2004, p. 7).

**Pune:** The Ambedkarites from all parts of the city were coming to the statue of Ambedkar and garlanding it. The residents of Bopodi, Dapodi, Indira Nagar, Dias Plot, Mangalwar Peth, etc., visited the statue in the morning to pay tribute. In the evening several programmes were organized in all parts of Pune (*Samrat,* 9th December 2004, p. 7). In Pimpri-Chinchwad, thousands of people gathered near the statue of Ambedkar to pay the tribute. The leaders of all political parties had joined the people. In most of the educational institutions of Pune, the people concerned with this field paid their tribute. (*Loksatta* (Pune), 7th December 2004, p. 2 and *Sakal* (Pune), 7th December 2004, p. 2).

**Mulund:** Candlelight march was organized (*Samrat,* 13th December 2004, p. 3).

**Mohol:** Tribute was paid by the Ambedkarites. All political parties having regard for Ambedkar's philosophy participated in the tribute ceremony (*Samrat,* 13th December 2004, p. 7).

**Vandre:** A candle march was arranged (*Samrat,* 7th December 2004, p. 3).

**Kolhapur:** Tributes were paid by the people by garlanding the statue of Ambedkar, near municipal corporation. Various programmes were organized in all parts of Kolhapur in the evening (*Pudhari* (Kolhapur), 7th December 2004).

All the local newspapers of Pune, Amaravati, Aurangabad, Akola, Nanded, Nagpur, Kolhapur, Nagar, Jalna, Sangli, Osmanabad, Nasik, etc., had highlighted the news of the 48th death anniversary of Ambedkar. In rural areas, the people garlanded the photo since the villages had no statues. On this day, i.e., on 6th December, every year programmes are being arranged in all parts of Maharashtra. This is an important day to spread awareness among the followers of Ambedkar.

## The Media and the 6th December

The media has been covering the celebrations of the 6th December. Amongst the media, every year, the local print media has been covering this event. The electronic media has been neglecting this important issue. This could be witnessed on the occasion of the 48th death anniversary of Ambedkar.

The print media had given satisfactory exposure to this occasion. Most of the local newspapers had given a good coverage of this tribute ceremony.

*Samrat,* a Marathi daily published from Dadar, Mumbai, is dedicated to Ambedkarite movement. The daily had published a special issue on the occasion of the death anniversary of Babasaheb Ambedkar. The special issue was titled as 'Samrat-Mahaparinirvana Din-2004' (*Samrat* Death Anniversary: A Special Issue 2004). It was in the form of a tabloid of 32 pages. The editor of the daily was Baban Kamble. The special issue contained select articles of eminent scholars. The titles of some articles were as (titles have been translated in English) Indian Politics in Independent India (by B.J. Kolse Patil), Ambedkar's Legal Fight (by J.V. Pawar), Ambedkarite Movement (by Chandrakumar Kamble), Ambedkar and Journalism (by Jayvanti Bhalshankar), etc. Above all, select speeches of Ambedkar were also published in this issue. Along with it, the interviews of Advocate Prakash Ambedkar and

Professor Jogendra Kawade (the leaders of two separate Republican parties) were given. The whole exercise was carried out to give direction to the Ambedkarite movement in Maharashtra. The *Samrat* had been covering the news on the death anniversary from 1st of December to around 19th December 2004. The news had been published along with photographs. This daily was dedicated to the Ambedkarite movement so it had covered the news to a great extent. In the issue of 7th December 2004, the daily had highlighted all the events of Ambedkarites at Chaityabhoomi with photographs and columns.

*Maharashtra Times*, a Marathi daily (Pune), had covered the news on its front page. The photograph of Ambedkarites was very attractive (see the issue of 7th December 2004). An editorial was also written on Ambedkar. Along with this, the local news were published on page 3.

*Loksatta*, a daily (Pune edition) had covered the news of the death anniversary of Ambedkar in its issue of 7th December 2004. A photograph of the people at Chaityabhoomi had been published on its front page and the details of the news had been given on page 4. The news was given in two columns. However, the tribute paid in Pune was highlighted by the daily on page 2. A local photograph was also published.

*Sakal*, a daily (Pune) had covered the news of Ambedkarites arrival at Chaityabhoomi (see the issue of 7th December 2004). A colour photograph of the people at Chaityabhoomi was published on its front page and the news was given on page 7. The news was given in four short columns. However, local news was published on page 2 with photograph of the local people.

*Sandhyakal*, an evening daily in Marathi published from Mumbai (editor-Rohini Khadilkar), had covered the news of the death anniversary (6th December 2004) on its front page with a colour photo of Ambedkar. The editorial had been written by the editor to pay tribute to Ambedkar. The editor explained the great work of Ambedkar and the improvement in the position of his people due to his work. According to the editor, there has been inflated ego and concentration of power among the Republican leaders, which is not letting them get united. If they or the people want to pay a real tribute to Ambedkar, all the groups of Republicans must come together. In this daily, three special articles were published to pay a tribute to Ambedkar. All the articles were expressing the activities and vision of Ambedkar and the present scenario.

*Mumbai Choufer* and *Mumbai-Dainik Sandhya*, both evening Marathi daily (Mumbai) had covered the news of the death anniversary function of Ambedkar (6th December 2004) and had paid tributes by writing editorials. The second daily had claimed that about 25 lakhs of people had visited the Chaityabhoomi. *Maha-Janashakti*, a Marathi daily (Mumbai, 6th December 2004), had paid a similar kind of tribute.

*Lokmat,* a Marathi daily had covered the news of the people at Chaityabhoomi. A colour photograph of Ambedkarites at Chaityabhoomi was published on the front page and the news was given in three short columns on page 2 (see the issue of 7th December 2004). In the issue of 6th December 2004, an article was published on Ambedkar and present position (by Ramakant Jadhav).

*Afternoon,* an English daily (Mumbai) had published just a photograph of Ambedkarites on the lower side of its front page. There was no news of the event (see the issue of 6th December 2004). Similar scant publicity was given by the *Indian Express,* an English daily (Pune) (see the issue of

7th December 2004, p. 4) whereas the *Times of India*, an English daily (Pune) had just published a local photograph from Pune without any news. There was no news or photo of Chaityabhoomi (see the issue of 7th December 2004, p. 3).

Summarily, it could be said that all the Marathi newspapers published from Mumbai had covered the news of the death anniversary of Ambedkar. Photographs were published and columns had been written whereas the local newspapers (from Pune) had published a photograph of the people at Chaityabhoomi with short columns. However, the local news had been covered in all the issues. Since these newspapers were regional, they had covered it. But in case of English newspapers, since their circulation is made on the national scale, some of them had given just a photo but no news columns were added. This is nothing but professionalism. The electronic media, i.e., *Sahyadri* had also covered the news. All the other professional channels had neglected the death anniversary of Ambedkar.

## Financial Grants for the Mahaparinirvana Din

Republican leaders and the other Ambedkarite leaders have been demanding financial grants from Municipal Corporation of Mumbai. The grants have been used for the arrangement of the facilities at Chaityabhoomi. Every year the amount of grant given has been Rs 3 lakh. Compared to the size of the crowd arriving at Chaityabhoomi, this grant seems to be very negligible. For the better arrangement of the facilities and the stalls, the leaders have made some suggestions to the Municipal Corporation of Mumbai. On the occasion of the 49th death anniversary of Ambedkar, the Republican leaders had demanded a financial grant of Rs 25 lakh for the better arrangement of the facilities. The demand was made in the meeting, which was called on 7th November 2005, at the Municipal Corporation of Mumbai. Eknath Gaikwad, Ravindra Pawar, Shailesh Dhivar, Chandrakant Kasabe, Chandramani Tambe and others were present at the meeting (*Samrat*, 8th November 2005, p. 1). The allotment of the stalls is done through the public advertisement. The Republican leaders have been taking care of providing the service or facilities to the Ambedkarites at Chaityabhoomi. The grants of the Municipal Corporation have been negligible. Hence, a number of organizations, political parties and non-governmental organizations have been providing services to the people at their own cost. All of these service providers are the followers of Ambedkar. Since, these organizations have been taking a major share in the services, the death anniversary day has been successful.

## The Development of Chaityabhoomi

The Chaityabhoomi, where Ambedkar was cremated, is becoming an important place in Maharashtra and India. Every year several lakhs of people have been visiting it on the occasion of Ambedkar's death anniversary. Therefore, the available space or area of Chaityabhoomi is becoming inconvenient. Hence, the Government of Maharashtra is planning to develop and restructure the area around Chaityabhoomi. The construction of stupa has been sanctioned. However, the development process has to be cleared by the Central Environment Department since the area comes under CRZ law. The Government of Maharashtra has requested the concerned department to treat Chaityabhoomi as a special case in order to carry out the process of development. The Chief Minister of Maharashtra,

Vilasrao Deshmukh has communicated the department to give no objection certificate for the proposed planning (*Sakal,* 3rd December 2004, p. 3).

The Government of Maharashtra also has a proposal of acquiring the area of India United Mill or Indu Mill for the development of Chaityabhoomi. The development in this regard has been at a satisfactory level. The government has appointed a committee for the reconstruction of stupa at Chaityabhoomi. Some of the members are Chandrakant Handore (Minister for the Social Justice, Government of Maharashtra), Dayanand Mhaske (Minister for the Housing Development), Eknath Gaikwad (Member of Parliament), T.M. Kamble (ex-member of Legislative Assembly) and others.

In this regard, a meeting of the committee members was called by Vilasrao Deshmukh, the Chief Minister of Maharashtra, to discuss the reconstruction of the stupa at Chaityabhoomi. The meeting was called at Sahyadri Guest House, Mumbai. The Chief Minister was also the Chairman. Bhante Rahul Bodhi (the monk), R.R. Patil (Deputy Chief Minister, Government of Maharashtra), Joney Joseph (Commissioner), Dayanand Mhaske (minister in Maharashtra government), Datta Salavi (Mayor of Mumbai), Ramdas Kadam (Leader of Opposition), Chandrakant Handore (minister in Maharashtra government), Meeratai Ambedkar (Chairman, the Buddhist Society of India), T.M. Kamble (ex-MLA) and others were present. The decision about the reconstruction of stupa and the development of Chaityabhoomi was taken by the committee (*Samrat*, 22 October 2005, p. 1). 'In coming one and half years, the financial arrangement of about 15 crore will be made available for the reconstruction of stupa. In the last phase, the area of Indu Mill will be taken by the government and will be used to reconstruct and develop the Chaityabhoomi' (*Sakal*, a daily (Pune), 22 October 2005, p. 16).

There have been various opinions and demands over the reconstruction and promotion of Chaityabhoomi. The most important demand of the Ambedkarites is that the Chaityabhoomi must be declared as a national monument. The Government of Maharashtra has considered this demand. Anand Mhaske, a minister in Maharashtra government, has objected at the slow speed of the work being carried out at Chaityabhoomi. He said that, 'the work has been very slow, it should be speeded up. The architecture, which is being constructed, is based on Hindu culture whereas it should be of Buddhist culture'. The minister has also demanded to use Buddhist architecture for the reconstruction of Chaityabhoomi. The art and painting at this place must explain the life and mission of Ambedkar so that the foreigners must come across this easily (*Samrat*, 6th November 2005, p. 8).

Eknath Gaikwad (Member of Parliament) has demanded to declare the Chaityabhoomi as an international monument. Bharat Integrated Reconstruction and Development Foundation (BIRD Foundation) had arranged a meeting at Mumbai. The meeting was chaired by Eknath Gaikwad. The members of the foundation are Bhadant Mahasthvir Rahu Bodhi, J.K. Kamble, Raj Gharade and others. The BIRD Foundation has passed some resolutions. Some of them are:

1. The Chaityabhoomi should be declared as an international monument.
2. The monument must be constructed during a definite period and the period must be declared now.

3. The master plan of the monument must be prepared and be given to all the concerned people.
4. The speed of the work at Chaityabhoomi should be speeded up.
5. The area of about 7.5 acres of Indu Mill should be given to the monument.

The Foundation has been monitoring the process of reconstruction of Chaityabhoomi (*Samrat,* 5th November 2005, p. 3).

As for the declaration of Chaityabhoomi as a national movement, there have been a number of rumours going on among the followers of Ambedkar about the authority. The responsibility of the Chaityabhoomi would be given to whom? This is the most common question among the people. At present, the responsibility is taken by the Buddhist Society of India. But, some of the political leaders of Republican Party of India also have an interest in this matter. Hence, the matter is becoming political. The media has reported that Prakash Ambedkar, the grandson of Ambedkar, is also interested in this matter (*Loksatta*, Mumbai edition, 6th December 2005).

Since Chaityabhoomi is located on the bank of the sea, there has been danger of its being inundated. The sea tides have been hitting the back wall compound and the stupa as well. When the sea level increases, the matter becomes serious. Already, the wall compound is damaged. Hence, there must be proper arrangement for the safety of the Chaityabhoomi.

The development of the Chaityabhoomi would be carried out in three stages as given below. The first stage has already begun. The three stages will be completed in the coming few years (*Loksatta*, Mumbai, 6th December 2005).

***First Stage***

- Construction of a road (around 140 metres) from Sant Dnyaneshwar to Chaityabhoomi with granite, marble and the Jaisalmer stone.
- Entry gate with big columns, the height of which would be 22 metres.
- Construction of Ashok Stambha, the height of which would be 19 metres.

***Second Stage***

- Reconstruction of stupa and the surrounding area.
- Construction of meditation centre.
- Electrification of Chaityabhoomi with attractive lights.

***Third Stage***

- Transferring the area or land of Indu Mill to Chaityabhoomi as part of its development.
- The land/area owned by the Municipal Corporation of Mumbai would also be transferred towards the Chaityabhoomi as part of its development programme.

The most important factor in the reconstruction and the development of the Chaityabhoomi is that the Ambedkarites, both the leaders and the people must take responsibility in these matters. There should not be politics or the tug of war situation in the process of development. The ultimate objective of the Ambedkarites is the development of the Chaityabhoomi and declaring it as a national monument.

The Government of Maharashtra, under the leadership of Vilasrao Deshmukh (the Chief Minister), had approached the central government on the matter of rebuilding and beautifying the Chaityabhoomi. The rebuilding and beautification work of Chaityabhoomi would speed up after the clearance from the Union Ministry. The Chief Minister had already obtained the clearance from A. Raja, the Environment Minister. Deshmukh, CM, had pleaded with the minister that, 'the issue should be looked at from the public sentiments, instead of bringing too much of rules in the picture. The construction work at Chaityabhoomi should be allowed by relaxing the CRZ regulations as the work involved a place of historical importance for public use and religious purpose' (Udwala, 2005).

The reconstruction and beautification of Chaityabhoomi has been designed by Shahi Prabhu, an architect and associate to the Unity Infra Project Company. According to the Company, 'the present stupa, which is in a dilapidated state will be demolished to make way for a bigger stupa. It will also be earthquake resistant. It also includes a big hall inside to accommodate the large number of visitors, who visit the Chaityabhoomi. At the entrance, a majestic torna will be built along the lines of the one at Sarnath. The pavements on the road leading to the main stupa will be beautified' (Nandy, 2004).

### *Main Features of the Project at Chaityabhoomi*

The construction work for the project has already begun. It includes mainly the reconstruction and the beautification. However, 'the beautification project had sparked off a controversy, when Dadar resident Geeta Padiwala filed a public interest litigation against certain design aspects of the project, which she said encroached into the sea. However, the Bombay High Court gave a go-ahead to the project in January and asked the project authorities to stay within the given direction' (ibid.). The main features of the project are as follows:

- ***Ashok Stambha***: A 60-feet-long concrete structure will be built. The first nine feet from the ground will have granite slabs. The next nine feet will have seven bronze lotus petals in oxidized bronze. The 27 feet will be clad in a copper sheet. At the top, a bronze Ashoka emblem will be provided.
- ***Torna:*** The structure will be about 21 metres high. It will be covered in glass reinforced concrete.
- ***A new stupa:*** A new, bigger stupa with a hall inside for visitors will replace the existing one. It will have marble exteriors and will be earthquake-resistant.
- Beautification of the pavements at the site (ibid.).

The Ambedkarites have been demanding that the Chaityabhoomi be declared as a national monument for the last several years. In the year 2003–2004, Atal Bihari Vajpayee, the Prime Minister of India, had said on the occasion of the 107th birth anniversary of Ambedkar that, 'As promised in the National Agenda, we will soon initiate measures to build a befitting national monument in honour of Ambedkar at his samadhi in Chaityabhoomi, Mumbai, on the lines of Raj Ghat in New Delhi' (Press Information Bureau, 2003). In the later period, the Ambedkarites' leaders went with the same demand to the government, but so far the Chaityabhoomi has not been declared as a national monument. However, the process is being carried out by the Central and the state government.

## Conclusion

The death anniversary of Ambedkar or the Mahaparinirvana Din of Ambedkar has been an important occasion in the life of Ambedkar's followers. Lakhs of people from all parts of India, especially from Maharashtra, have been visiting the

Chaityabhoomi in order to pay tribute to Ambedkar. One could notice the unique spirit among the Ambedkar's people. Despite continuous travel for around two days, and having been thirsty and hungry, the first preference of the people was to pay tribute to Ambedkar. They were staying in long queue and were waiting for about 5 hours with enthusiastic expressions. Significant number of people were also paying their tribute at the shore of sea or on one side of Chaityabhoomi. The spirit, the love, the attachment and the commitment of the people on this day was remarkable. Similar kind of trend could be found among a number of organizations, which were serving the people. There were social, political and cultural organizations dedicated to Ambedkarite movement helping the people. Every organization was trying to provide some service to the followers of Ambedkar who had arrived at Chaityabhoomi. From drinking water, breakfast, meal to medical service, various kinds of services were made available free of cost. Lakhs of Ambedkar's people have benefited from these services. The responsibility and the social commitment of the organizations was remarkable. The area around Chaityabhoomi from Shivaji Park to Dadar, all the roads were overflowing with people. This was the response of Ambedkar's people on the occasion of death anniversary of Ambedkar even after 48 years. This shows how important Ambedkar still is.

## References

Nandy, Madhura (2004) on www.chalomumbai.com, 10–04–2004.

Press Information Bureau (PIB) on www.pib.nic.com.

Singh, Sarina et. al. (2003), *Lonely Planet: India*, Lonely Planet Publication, London.

Tarun, Udwala (2005) on www.mailarchieve.com-news, 21 May, 2005.

Turner, Barry (2005), *The Statesman's Yearbook*, Palgrave Publication, London.

### *Newspapers*

*Samrat* (Marathi), a daily dedicated to Ambedkarite movement, Mumbai.

*Maharashtra Times* (Marathi), Pune.

*Loksatta* (Marathi), Pune.

*Sakal* (Marathi), Pune.

*Sandhyakal* (Marathi), Mumbai.

*Mumbai Chowfer* (Marathi), Mumbai.

*Mumbai Dainik* (Marathi), Mumbai.

*Lokamat* (Marathi), Pune.

*Afternoon* (English), Mumbai.

*Indian Express* (English), Pune.

*Times of India* (English), Pune.

# Chapter 9

# Ambedkarites' Socio-Cultural Transformation

In the last phase of the life of Babasaheb Ambedkar, a revolutionary event took place. This was the beginning of the intellectual war. Ambedkar wanted to bring Buddhism in India to eradicate the caste system. In this effort, he was attending a number of conferences and meets dedicated to Buddhism. He was also thinking of writing a book on Buddhism. Long before, in 1935 at Yevla, he had declared that, 'Though I am born a Hindu, I do not intend to die a Hindu'. In December 1954, Ambedkar attended the Third Buddhist World Conference at Rangoon. At that time, his health was critical yet he attended the conferences on Buddhism in Sri Lanka (1950), Rangoon (1954) and Nepal (1956). In Nepal, he delivered a lecture on 'Buddhism and Communism'. Despite his ill-health, he was attending these conferences and also wrote an important book titled as *The Buddha and His Dhamma*. Ambedkar embraced Buddhism on 14th October 1956. His followers also have embraced Buddhism. The Ambedkarites or the Buddhists in Maharashtra have undergone a cultural transformation. The Mahars of Maharashtra accepted Buddhism and are practising Buddhist culture. The Ambedkarites have created a new social identity. This chapter seeks to explain the cultural transformation of the Ambedkarites in Maharashtra.

**The Mahars: An Overview**

The origin of the caste Mahar is considered by many scholars. According to R.E. Enthoven (1922, reprinted in 1990: 401), 'The origin of the term Mahar is said to be derived from Mahahari or the great eater, in support of which a few traditions are quoted below. According to others, it is derived through Prakrit from the Sanskrit work, *Mritahari,* which is given as the name of the lowest caste. In the Puranas they are also called *Mritaharins*. This name they are said to have earned by their occupation of removing carcasses of dead animals'.

Enthoven has given 53 endogamous divisions among the Mahars. Out of these, in some divisions of the Mahars, they could eat together but cannot intermarry (ibid., 405). Some important divisions of the Mahars as cited by Enthoven are given below:

| | | |
|---|---|---|
| Abne | Bavcha | Bunkar |
| Balkmble | Bavise | Dhed |
| Ghadshi | Kasare | Mathkamble |
| Murli | Rali | Soma or Somavanshi |
| Sonakamble | Tiltam | |

He has also given some surnames of the Mahars. Some of them are:

| | | |
|---|---|---|
| Adhav | Ahire | Adsule |
| Auchat | Bagul | Bhalerao |
| Bhosale | Dukare | Gaikwad |
| Jadhav | Kadam | Kamble |

| | |
|---|---|
| Kharat | Sonkamble |
| Sonavane | Waghmare |

According to Enthoven, the Mahars profess Hinduism. The favourite deities of the Mahars are Khandoba, Vithoba, Mhasoba, Satvai, Mariai, etc. (ibid., 413). Further, the author has given brief accounts about their place of residence and untouchability. The author writes that, 'The Mahars live outside villages in special Mharwadas or Mahar quarters. Their houses are generally untidy and ill cared, made of mud and stone with thatched roofs' (ibid., 402). Further, the author writes that, 'The Mahars are held to be impure … the village barber will not shave the Mahars, nor are they allowed to draw water from the village well … a pot was hung from their necks to hold their spittle, they were made to drag thorns to wipe out their footsteps. And when a Brahmin comes near, were forced to lie far off on their faces lest their shadow might fall on him' (ibid., 402). The author's description gives an idea about the nature and life of the Maharas. They were treated as untouchables. They used to live with a number of social restrictions. Inhuman treatment was meted out to them.

Over the years, the social and economic condition of the Mahars had remained inhuman and worse. There was no improvement in any constructive way. After the agitations of Ambedkar, the Mahars and the other untouchable castes had been given some safeguards. Ambedkar's efforts brought improvement in the condition of the Mahars and the other untouchables. The Mahars became ardent followers of Ambedkar. Basically, Ambedkar too belonged to the Mahar community. He sacrificed his whole life for the social and economic upliftment of the Mahars and the untouchables. Finally, Ambedkar took a decision to convert to Buddhism. The decision of conversion was revolutionary, although he had declared the decision of conversion long back in 1935 at Yevla. In May 1956, his talk on Buddhism was broadcast by BBC, London. Ambedkar said that, 'I prefer Buddhism because it gives three principles in combination, which no other religion does. Buddhism teaches *Prajna* (understanding as against superstition and supernaturalism), *Karuna* (love) and *Samata* (equality). This is what man wants for a good and happy life. Neither God nor soul can save society' (Keer, 1971: 490). On 14th October 1956, Ambedkar embraced Buddhism and along with him several lakhs of Mahars too embraced Buddhism. Since then, the Mahars are moving through a cultural transformation. The Mahars are now Buddhists. They are not a part of Hindu caste system. They have created a perfect social and cultural identity. The socio-cultural transformation of the Buddhists or Ambedkarites could be found in the social and individual functions or ceremonies.

## Vows: The Essential Part of Buddhism

The Mahars of Maharashtra have accepted and are practising Buddhism. Every Buddhist remembers the 22 vows formulated by Ambedkar. The vows are rational. These are given below:

1. I shall have no faith in Brahma, Vishnu and Mahesh nor shall worship them.
2. I shall have no faith in Rama and Krishna who are believed to be the incarnation of God nor shall I worship them.
3. I shall have no faith in Gauri, Ganapati and the other gods and goddesses of Hindus nor shall I worship them.
4. I do not believe in the incarnation of God.

5. I do not and shall not believe that Lord Buddha was the incarnation of Vishnu. I believe this to be sheer madness and false propaganda.
6. I shall not perform shraadh nor shall I give pindam.
7. I shall not act in a manner violating the principles and teaching of the Buddha.
8. I shall not allow any ceremonies to be performed by Brahmins.
9. I shall believe in the equality of man.
10. I shall endeavour to establish equality.
11. I shall follow the noble eightfold path of the Buddha.
12. I shall follow the ten parameters prescribed by the Buddha.
13. I shall have compassion and loving kindness for all living beings and protect them.
14. I shall not steal.
15. I shall not tell lies.
16. I shall not commit carnal sins.
17. I shall not take intoxicants like liquor, drugs, etc.
18. I shall endeavour to follow the noble eightfold path and practise compassion and loving kindness in every day life.
19. I renounce Hinduism, which is harmful for humanity and impedes the advancement and development of humanity because it is based on inequality; and adopt Buddhism as my religion.
20. I firmly believe that the Dhamma of the Buddha is the only true religion.

21. I believe that I am having a re-birth.
22. I solemnly declare and affirm that I shall hereafter lead my life according to the principles and teachings of the Buddha and his Dhamma.

The above vows are the most important, which are administered to every Buddhist. The content of the vows can be expressed as they are anti-Hindu and pro-Buddhist. The vows teach the Buddhists to live with a rational and scientific outlook towards humanity and equality. As a result of these vows, the Buddhists are no longer following the Hindu culture, but they have created their own different culture, which is contrary to the Hindus. They do not worship Hindu gods, they do not go to temples, and they do not perform their ceremonies as per the Hindu culture or by the Brahmin priest. The Bhikus or the monks are performing the ceremonies of the Buddhists. There are also representatives of the Buddhist Society of India, who are performing such duties. It is a fact that there are some Buddhists who also abide by the Hindu culture. This is because; they have got cultural conflict. The religion of Buddhism as given by Ambedkar has completed 52 years, whereas the Hindu religion is hundreds of years old. Despite this small period, neo-Buddhism has achieved a lot.

### Jay Bhim: The Honour of Ambedkarites

Ambedkarites respect Ambedkar for his contribution and sacrifice. They respect him for having given them the gift of Buddhism, the new hope for life. In order to give honour to Ambedkar, Ambedkarites say Jay Bhim when they meet each other or when they communicate with each other. Jay Bhim means the victory to Bhim or victory to Ambedkar. It is surprising that, even after 52 years of the death of Ambedkar, his name and work is respected every moment by every Ambedkarite. This shows the love of Ambedkarites towards their leader. On Jay Bhim or the work of Ambedkar, several hundreds of poems have been written. These poems describe the work of Ambedkar. One poet Vilas Devare (1996) has given the deep meaning of Jay Bhim as below:

***What Does Jay Bhim Mean?***

Jai Bhim means light.

Jai Bhim means love.

Jai Bhim means a head blow to Chaturvarna.

Jai Bhim means a journey from darkness to light.

Jai Bhim means the tears in the eyes of millions.

Jai Bhim means a guiding light on the path to high ground.

Jai Bhim means the identity of a Dalit Buddhist.

Jai Bhim means knowledge.

Jai Bhim means a word that dislocates the bones of the Vedic religion.

Jai Bhim means a crack in the soul of those who break their own promises.

Jai Bhim means the end to the doing of those who betray the country in the name of religion.

Jai Bhim means a loud ringing that shatters the ears of those who think they are highborn.

Jai Bhim means the end of the stigma of untouchability.

Jai Bhim means a noose around the neck of those who have harmed society.

Jai Bhim means fruition of the idea of equality.

Jai Bhim means walkway to progress.

The meaning of Jay Bhim given by Vilas Devare is important since it represents the sentiments of the Ambedkarites. The Ambedkarites respect Ambedkar for giving them dignity, humanity, equality, etc. The victory of Bhim (Ambedkar) is against all odds created by the caste system. Ambedkar showed them a path of light and knowledge. Ambedkarites also respect Ambedkar for giving Buddhism to them. The Ambedkarites are thankful to Ambedkar for showing them the path of light. The way of the Buddha is the way of development. Therefore, in order to give tribute and honour to him, all Ambedkarites say Jay Bhim.

Over the years, the culture of the Buddhists is moving through the process of transformation. The nature of the social ceremonies of the Ambedkarites have changed. The Ambedkarites or the Buddhists have created a new culture. This new culture can be found in their names. Some of the examples of the names are Anand, Gunratna, Gautam, Prabuddha, Dhammaratna, Dhammakirti, Sangharatna, Pradnya, Sanghamitra, etc. The marriages and the other ceremonies are performed according to the Buddhist culture. The conversion to Buddhism has brought revolutionary changes among the Ambedkarites.

## Buddhism: A Path of Development

The Buddhists in Maharashtra have created a model of development. They have sacrificed their traditional occupations and have accepted education as the means of development. Ambedkar's message 'educate, agitate and organize' is followed by them. The Buddhism teaches equality and humanity. It has given self-respect and dignity to the Ambedkarites. This positive side of the Ambedkarites and the thoughts of Ambedkar have attracted other people from different castes. Large majority of the Buddhists are originally from the Mahar caste. But, recently the Matangs have also converted to Buddhism. Interestingly, the leader of the nomadic tribes, Laxman Mane embraced Buddhism in October 2006. He was impressed with the teaching of Buddhism and the development of the Ambedkarites. He decided to convert the nomadic tribes to Buddhism. Finally, on the occasion of the 50th anniversary of Ambedkar's conversion, he organized a mass conversion ceremony in Mumbai on 27th May 2008. 'On this occasion more than one lakh Dalits and tribal Hindus embraced Buddhism. This is the largest mass conversion in the country after 1956' (*The Hindu:* 2007). This conversion ceremony was jointly organized and supported by the Republican Party of India. This conversion ceremony shows the importance of Buddhism. Many people are attracted towards this religion.

## Conclusion

The Ambedkarites or the Buddhists are moving through a socio-cultural transformation. They have established their new social identity. The Buddhists do not like to call themselves as a part of Hindu society. They do not recognize them as the Mahars too. They try to follow the ideology of Ambedkar. However, there seems to be a dilemma about the culture. This is because of the limitations that existed in the application and implementation of the teaching of Buddhism. After embracing the Buddhism in 1956, Ambedkar's death took place within two months. This was a huge setback for all the Ambedkarites. However, the Buddhist Society of India and other Buddhist organizations are working devotedly for the spread of the ideals set forth by Ambedkar.

## References


Devare Vilas (1996), *"Jai Bhim Mhanaje Kay?"*, Published in *Maitrani*, Marathi journal published by Moon Meenakshi.

Zelliot, Eleanor (2001) "The Meaning of Ambedkar" in Ghanshyam Shah (2001), *Dalit Identity and Politics*, Sage Publication, New Delhi.

Enthoven, R.E. (1922, reprinted in 1990), *The Tribes and Castes of Bombay*, Asian Educational Services, New Delhi.

Keer, Dhananjay (1954, 1971, reprinted), *Ambedkar: Life and Mission*, Popular Prakashan, Bombay.

*The Hindu:* 2007, 28 May, (see www.hindu.com).

# Bibliography


Agricultural Census (2000), Government of India Publication.

*Ambedkar Babasaheb: Writings and Speech*, Vol. I, Department of Education, Government of Maharashtra Publication, Mumbai.

*Ambedkar Babasaheb: Writings and Speech*, Vol. II, Government of Maharashtra Publication.

Chalam, K.S. (1993) (ed.), *Relevance of Ambedkarism in India*, Rawat Publications, New Delhi, Jaipur.

Cohen, R.L. (1956), *The Economics of Agriculture*, Cambridge University Press, London.

Devare, Vilas (1996), "Jai Bhim Mhanaje Kay?", Published in *Maitrani*, a Marathi journal published by Moon Meenakshi.

Dolas, Avinash (1995), *Marathi Dalit Katha*, Savita Prakashan, Aurangabad.

Economic Survey (2006–07), Government of India Publication, New Delhi.

Economic Survey (2000–2001), Government of India Publication.

Eleventh Five-Year Plan (2007–12), Vol. I, Government of India Publication, New Delhi.

Enthoven, R.E. (1922, reprinted in 1990), *The Tribes and Castes of Bombay*, Asian Educational Services, New Delhi.

Five Year Plan (2002–2007), Vol. II, Planning Commission, Government of India.

Grover, Virender (Ed.) (1993), *B.R. Ambedkar: Political Thinker of Modern India*, Deep and Deep Publication, New Delhi.

Gunnar, Myrdal (1968), *Asian Drama*, Vol. II

Harold, Issac (1965), *India's Ex-untouchables*, Asia Publishing House, Bombay.

Jadhav, Raja (2000), *Saha December 1956 and Nantar*, Granthali Prakashan, Mumbai.

Jadhav, Praveen (2008), *Ambedkar's People in India*, Rajat Publication, New Delhi.

Kamble, J.R. (1979), *Rise and Awakening of Depressed Classes in India*, National Publishing House, New Delhi.

Kamble, N.D. (1982), *The Scheduled Castes*, Ashish Publishing House, New Delhi.

Kantowsky, Dentlief (2003), *Buddhists in India Today: Description, Pictures and Documents*, Manohar Publication, New Delhi.

Keer, Dhananjay (1954, reprinted 1971), *Ambedkar: Life and Mission*, Popular Prakashan, Bombay.

Khan, Mumtaz Ali (1980), *Scheduled Castes and their Position in India*, Uppal Publishing House, New Delhi.

Madhura, Nandy (2004) on www.chalomumbai.com, 10 April, 2004.

Naik, C.D. (2003), *Thoughts and Philosophy of Dr B.R. Ambedkar*, Sarup and Sons, New Delhi.

Nimbalkar, Waman (1990), *Ambedkari Vicharanchi Disha*, Prabodhan Prakashan, Nagpur.

Nurkse, Ragnar (1953), *Problems of Capital Formation in Underdeveloped Countries*, Oxford University Press, London.

Panikkar, K.M. (1955), *Hindu Society at the Crossroads*, Asia Publishing House, Bombay.

Paul, P. (2006), *Security Research Review*, (www.bharat-rakshak.com).

Press Information Bureau (PIB) on www.pib.nic.com

Ramesh Chandra and Sangh Mittra (2003), *The Ambedkar Era*, Commonwealth Publishers, New Delhi.

Sada, Karhade (1992), *Marxwad, Buddhawad Aani Ambedkarwad*, Granthali Prakashan, Mumbai.

Sadhu, A.N. and Amarjit Singh (1998), *Fundamentals of Agricultural Economics*, Himalaya Publishing House, New Delhi, p. 202.

Saini, G.G. (1979), *Farm Size, Resource Use, Efficiency and Income Distribution*, Allied Publication, New Delhi.

Sen, Amartya (1964), "*Size of Holdings and Productivity*", *Economic & Political Weekly*, Vol. 16, February, 1964. [also see, Sen Amartya (1964), "An Aspect of Indian Agriculture", *Economic & Political Weekly*, Vol. 4, Feb.1964.]

Singh, Sarina et al. (2003), *Lonely Planet: India*, Lonely Planet Publication, London.

Social Welfare Committee for SCs/STs Report 1999–2000, Government of India.

Tenth Five-Year Plan Proceedings (2002–2007), Government of India Publication, New Delhi.

The Buddhist Society of India (2004), *Bouddhanchi Pavitra Sthale*, A booklet, published by The Buddhist Society of India.

Thomas, Edgar (1960), *An Introduction to Agricultural Economics*, Nelson Press, New York.

Turner, Barry (2005), *The Statesman's Yearbook*, Palgrave Publication, London.

Udwala, Tarun (2005) on www.mailarchieve.com news, 21 May, 2005.

Wankhede, G.G. (2001), Educational Inequalities among Scheduled Castes in Maharashtra, *EPW*, May 5, 2001.

Zelliot, Eleanor (2001) "The Meaning of Ambedkar" in Ghanshyam Shah (2001), *Dalit Identity and Politics*, Sage Publication, New Delhi.

Zutshi, Ravi (1994), "Enhancing India's Competitive Position through Agro-industrial Development", *Indian Journal of Public Administration*, Vol. XL, No. 2, April-June, 1994.

### *Newspapers*

*Afternoon* (English), Mumbai.

*Indian Express,* (English), Pune.

*Lokamat,* (Marathi), Pune.

*Loksatta,* (Marathi), Pune.

*Maharashtra Times* (Marathi), Pune.

*Mumbai Chowfer,* (Marathi), Mumbai.

*Mumbai Dainik,* (Marathi), Mumbai.

*Sakal,* (Marathi), Pune.

*Samrat,* (Marathi) a daily dedicated to Ambedkarite Movement, Mumbai'.

*Sandhyakal,* (Marathi), Mumbai.

*Times of India,* (English), Pune.

# Appendix

## Selected Quotes of Dr Babasaheb Ambedkar on Conversion

[Dr B.R. Ambedkar embraced Buddhism on 14th October 1956 at Nagpur (Maharashtra). His millions of followers also embraced Buddhism. On the next day, i.e., on 15th October 1956, he delivered a speech at the same place, which is now known as Diksha Bhoomi. Some important passages from Dr Ambedkar's speech on the conversion have been given here. The 14th October of every year is celebrated as Dhamma Chakra Pravartana Din.]

**The Selection of Place (Nagpur) for the Conversion**

'Now, the first question that occupies the mind of many is, why should the choice of venue fall on Nagpur? Some people believe that, I have purposely chosen this place because this city is the centre of Rashtriya Swayamsevak Sangh (RSS) activities and that I wanted to do something spectacular right in front of their eyes. Well, that is not true. I have no such motive. I have no desire to irritate or to provoke anybody by scratching his nose nor do I have time for these kind of childish pranks'.

'Some people are under the impression that another reason why I chose this place and this time for the initiation ceremony was because on the same day and at the same time Rashtriya Swayamsevak Sangh was holding a rally in Nagpur. This ceremony, was intended to juxtapose a striking contrast. That of course, is not true. Why should we go out of our way to quarrel with the RSS? We have no time to do so, nor does it deserve that honour'.

### The Reason for Selecting Nagpur City for the Conversion Ceremony

'Those who have studied the Buddhist history of India, know that the people who worked in the beginning for the propagation of the religion of Buddha were the Nagas. Nagas were non-Aryans and there existed fierce enmity between the Aryans and the Naga. Many a battle was fought between the Aryans and the non-Aryans. Aryans wanted to completely annihilate the Nagas. There are many legends to be found in the Puranas in this connection. Aryans had burnt Nagas. The Sage Agastya saved one Naga and we are supposed to be the descendants of that Naga. The Nagas were suppressed and oppressed by the Aryans. They needed a great man to liberate them and they found that, great man in the form of Lord Buddha. Bhagwan Buddha saved them from decay and extinction. It was the Nagas who spread the religion of the Buddha throughout the world. These people were predominantly the inhabitants of Nagpur. Through the soil of this city there flowed a river named the Nag. It appears that the Nagas lived on the banks of this river. This is mainly the reason for selecting Nagpur for this great occasion. There is no other reason. The choice of this city conducting Deeksha-initiation ceremony need not cause any misunderstanding'.

### Answer to the Objections Raised by the Hindus

'Their (Hindu critics) objection pertains to the removal of the dead bodies of animals. Mahars and Chamars stopped removing the dead bodies of buffaloes and cows. Mahars and Chamars do not eat carrion was a slogan raised by me. Some thirty years ago I launched this movement. This somehow immensely offended our Hindu friends. I asked them, "you take the milk from the cows and buffaloes and when they are dead you expect us to remove the dead bodies. Why? If you carry the dead bodies of your mothers to cremate, why do not carry the dead bodies of your mother-cows; yourself?". When I put this question to the Hindus they felt irritated. I told them, if you let us remove the dead bodies of your mothers, we shall very gladly remove the dead bodies of your cows and buffaloes as well. Many letters written by the Brahmins and other Hindu correspondents appeared in the *Kesari*. A Chitpavan Brahmin through, one of such letters tried to prove that if the untouchables stopped removing the dead bodies of animals they would be put to a great financial loss. He argued his point by furnishing statistical data in support of his argument. According to him every Chamar who removed the dead bodies of the animals earned between Rs 500 to Rs 600 per annum from the sale proceeds of the skin, teeth, hoofs and bones of the dead cows. He accused me that, I was trying to deprive them of their livelihood by preaching against this practice. My people were in a dilemma not knowing where I was leading them. Once I happened to visit Sangmaner – a tehsil of the district of Belgaum. The author of those letters, which had appeared in the *Kesari* met me and repeated the same question. I told him that, I would answer this question some time later. Then I answered this question in a public meeting in this manner'.

'Many people do not have sufficient food to eat. Women have no clothes to cover their bodies. No roof over their heads to give them shelters. No land to grow food – grains. So they are downtrodden and poverty-stricken. They are oppressed and exploited. Do you know the reason why? None replied from among the congregation. Not even the man who had written those letters to the *Kesari*. Then I told them, you had better, leave us alone. Good men, we are quite capable of thinking for ourselves. If you are so much anxious about our losses why not send your friends and relative to live in the villages and do this dirty job of dragging the dead bodies of animals so that they may earn Rs 500 per annum. In addition to that amount I will pay Rs 500 from my pocket. They will gain doubly. Why miss this opportunity? True, we will suffer a loss but you stand to gain'.

'Unfortunately nobody has come forward to claim the prize so far. Why on earth do they feel perturbed on seeing us making progress? I can take care of my people for the food, clothing, houses and other things they need. You (Hindus) need not worry about these things. If we do this dirty work, it is said to be profitable and if you do it, it becomes non-profitable. Strange logic it is, isn't it?'

### About the Media (Newspaper)

'I do not know what sort of publicity will be given to my speech by the newspapers of our country. I do not care for publicity very much but these newspapermen have been after me for the past forty years. They have maligned me. They have misrepresented my views. They have mutilated my speeches. I wish these newspapermen could learn to behave like mature people, and to think and write in a responsible and truthful manner so that the world may know the truth and form a better impression about them'.

### The Reason for Embracing Buddhism

'The question of our conversion is being discussed everywhere, but I am surprised to see that nobody has asked me the reason why of all the religions I have chosen the religion of Buddha. In movement of conversion this is a significant question to be asked. At the time of embracing a religion one should ask oneself these questions, namely:

1. Which religion should be adopted?
2. And how it should be adopted?

I started the movement of renouncing the Hindu religion in 1935 at Nasik and since then I have been continuing the struggle. A mammoth meeting was held at Yevala, in 1935 in which through a resolution a decision was taken to the effect that we should renounce the Hindu religion. In that meeting, I had said that though born a Hindu, because I could not help it, I would not die as a Hindu. This conversion has given me enormous satisfaction and unimaginable pleasure. I feel as if I have been liberated from hell. I want each one of you all who got initiated yesterday, to realise this by his own experience. But I do not want any blind followers. I do not like sheep mentality. Those who wish to come under the refuge of Buddha should do so after counting the cost, for it is a religion very difficult to practice'.

### The Enthusiasm and the Hindu Society

'Why does the human mind become diseased? The reason is so that so long as the human body is not free from suffering, mind cannot be happy. There is a saying by Ramdas, the Maharashtrian saint, that if a man lacks enthusiasm either his mind or body is in a diseased condition. Now, what says about the enthusiasm in man? If there is no enthusiasm, life becomes a drudgery – a mere burden to be dragged. Nothing can be achieved if there is no enthusiasm. Why does one lose enthusiasm? Main reason for this lack of enthusiasm on the part of a man is that, an individual loses hope to get an opportunity to elevate oneself. Hopelessness leads to lack of enthusiasm. The mind in such cases becomes diseased'.

'For inspiration and enthusiasm one must have a healthy and sound mind. Such a man is capable of surmounting all kinds of difficulties. He has confidence, courage and will to rise and that gives him the inspiration and enthusiasm.'

'Unfortunately, Hinduism, which is founded on the ideologies of inequality and injustice, leaves no room for the development of enthusiasm. So long as the untouchable continue to be slave under the yoke of Hinduism, a diabolical creed, they can have no hope, no inspiration, no enthusiasm for better life. They might produce no more than a few hundred clerks, poor clerks, who will do nothing excepting filling their bellies. What else can they do? Then we shall need super-clerks to protect them from injustice and various kinds of atrocities. Common masses of the untouchables will not gain anything. The Scheduled Castes can never feel enthusiastic about the inspiration they derive from Hinduism'.

## Foreign Scholarship to Scheduled Castes

'Lord Linlithgow agreed to my suggestion and the result was that 16 boys belonging to the Scheduled Castes were sent abroad for higher education. Out of these sixteen, some took full advantage of this opportunity and others did not. They got only half-baked and returned home. The reason is that there exists no enthusiasm for the Scheduled Castes in

Hinduism, though such an atmosphere exists for the Brahmins and other castes'.

## Caste System and Its Consequences

'Besides the lack of congenial atmosphere there is also lack of equality among Hindus. This religion and this social order have ruined us. But this is not going to stop here. This would ruin the Hindus themselveṣ and ultimately India. I do not accuse the Hindu religion in vain. This religion cannot save anybody. It has no life left in it. Why has our country lost her freedom time and again? Why have we been subjected to foreign domination so often? It is because this country as a whole never stood against the enemy. It was always a small section of the society and whoever overpowered it became the victor. This is mainly due to the pernicious caste system of the Hindus'.

'Hinduism cannot save anybody. There is no salvation for anybody in Hinduism. According to the tenants of Hinduism, only the so-called higher castes have been benefited. There is no exaggeration in my statement. What have the Sudras or the untouchables gained?'

'As soon as the wife of a Brahmin man conceives, she thinks of the High Court, whether any post of a judge has fallen vacant or not, but when our woman becomes pregnant, she cannot think of anything better than a sweeper's post under the Municipal Committee'.

## The Need of Buddhism

'The fundamental principle of Buddhism is equality. Of all the Bhikkus, who joined the Order in the time of Lord Buddha about 75 per cent of the Bhikkus belonged to the Brahmins and remaining 25 per cent were the Sudras. Even then "Buddhism" was called the religion of the Sudras'.

> 'O ! Bhikkus !, you belong to different castes and have come from various lands. Just as the great rivers when they have fallen into the great ocean lose their identity just so, O brethren, do these four castes, Kshatriyas, Brahmins, Vaishyas, Sudras; when they begin to follow the doctrine and discipline as propounded by the Tathagata, they renounce different names of castes and rank and becomes members of one and the same society'.
>
> —Lord Buddha

'There was only one man who raised his voice against the separatism and untouchability and that was Lord Buddha. In the beginning Lord Buddha got only ten or twelve Bhikkus. Out of these nine or ten were Sudras. This is evident from the autobiographical Gathas of the Bhikkus entitled as *Thera Gatha* and *Therigatha*. Their writings bear testimony to the fact that Buddhism is the only religion, which does not recognise caste and affords full scope for progress'.

'Some people will naturally ask this question, what will the untouchables gain by embracing Buddhism? Suffice this to say that it is a worthless question'.

'Is religion necessary for the well to do? No, perhaps not. Those who are holding high positions in life, have nice bungalows to live in, money to buy all comforts of life and servants to attend on them, perhaps, have little use for religion'.

'We shall go ahead undoubtedly on the path we have chosen. We have found a new way to life and we shall follow it. This path leads to progress. In fact, this is not something new nor have we imported it from outside. Buddhism is the religion of this country. It is more than two thousand years old. I feel sorry for the fact that, I did not embrace this religion earlier'.

### The Teachings of Buddha

'The teachings of the Buddha are eternal but even then Buddha did not proclaim them to be infallible. The religion of Buddha has the capacity to change according to times, a quality, which no other religion can claim to have'.

'The principles and teaching of "Bhagwan Buddha" are eternal but in spite of this fact, Buddha did not claim any status for himself, nor did he claim principles to be infallible. He never claimed divinity for his self or for his religion. Buddha did not say that he was the Son of God or the last prophet-messenger of God. On the contrary he said, my father and my mother are ordinary mortals'.

Buddhism denies the existence of God and soul. The real basis of Buddhism is a rational way to eradicate suffering. 'There is widespread suffering in the world', Buddha said. Ninety per cent of the people are afflicted with suffering or misery of some kind or the other. The main object of Buddhism is to emancipate the suffering humanity. The question arises, then what is the use of *Das Capital?* I believe that, Karl Marx was far behind Buddha, for he did not say anything that had not been brought to light by the Buddha himself, some two thousand and four hundred years before Marx was born.

*Note:* The author has given here some important quotes or parts of the speech of Dr Ambedkar, which was delivered on 15th October 1956. The intention of the author is to relate the speech with the content of the book. However, for the full text of the speech, the below source can be referred.

*Source:* Bhagwan Das (1969), *Thus Spoke Ambedkar: Selected Speeches*, Vols. I and II, Bheem Patrika, Jalandhar.

# Index